EVERYDAY FOODS IN WAR TIME

LECTOR HOUSE PUBLIC DOMAIN WORKS

EVERYDAY FOODS IN WAR TIME

MARY SWARTZ ROSE

ISBN: 978-93-5344-889-9

Published: 1918

© LECTOR HOUSE LLP

LECTOR HOUSE LLP
E-MAIL: lectorpublishing@gmail.com

EVERYDAY FOODS IN WAR TIME

BY

MARY SWARTZ ROSE

ASSISTANT-PROFESSOR, DEPARTMENT OF NUTRITION,
TEACHERS COLLEGE, COLUMBIA UNIVERSITY

1918

The time has come, the Aggies said,
To talk of many things,
Of what to eat, of calories,
Of cabbages and kings,
Of vitamines and sausages,
And whether costs have wings.

Journal of Home Economics,
November, 1917.

PREFACE

"FOOD IS FUEL FOR FIGHTERS. Do not waste it. Save WHEAT,
MEAT, SUGARS AND FATS. Send more to our Soldiers, Sailors
and Allies."

The patriotic housewife finds her little domestic boat sailing in uncharted waters. The above message of the Food Administration disturbs her ordinary household routine, upsets her menus and puts her recipes out of commission. It also renders inoperative some of her usual methods of economy at a time when rising food prices make economy more imperative than ever. To be patriotic and still live on one's income is a complex problem. This little book was started in response to a request for "a war message about food." It seemed to the author that a simple explanation of the part which some of our common foods play in our diet might be both helpful and reassuring. To change one's menu is often trying; to be uncertain whether the substituted foods will preserve one's health and strength makes adjustment doubly difficult. It is hoped that the brief chapters which follow will make it easier to "save wheat, meat, sugars and fats" and to make out an acceptable bill of fare without excessive cost.

Thanks are due to the Webb Publishing Company, St. Paul, Minnesota, for permission to reprint three of the chapters, which appeared originally in *The Farmer's Wife*.

TEACHERS COLLEGE,
Columbia University,
New York City.

December 1, 1917.

CONTENTS

EVERYDAY FOODS IN WAR TIME

CHAPTER I

THE MILK PITCHER IN THE HOME

(Reprinted from *The Farmer's Wife*, by permission of the Webb Publishing Company.)

There is a quaint old fairy tale of a friendly pitcher that came and took up its abode in the home of an aged couple, supplying them from its magic depths with food and drink and many other comforts. Of this tale one is reminded in considering the place of the milk pitcher in the home. How many housewives recognize the bit of crockery sitting quietly on the shelf as one of their very best friends? How many know that it will cover many of their mistakes in the choice of food for their families? That it contains mysterious substances upon which growth depends? That it stands ready to save them both work and worry in regard to food? That it is really the only indispensable article on the bill of fare?

Diet is like a house, a definite thing, though built of different kinds of material. For a house we need wall material, floor material, window, ceiling, chimney stuffs and so forth. We may, if we like, make floors, walls, and ceilings all of the same kind of stuff, wood for example, but we should need glass for windows and bricks or tile for chimneys. Or, again, we may choose brick for walls, floors, and chimneys but it would not do any better than wood for windows, would be rather unsatisfactory for ceilings, and impossible for doors. In other words, we could not build a modern house from one kind of material only and we really need at least four to carry out even a simple plan.

In a similar fashion, diet is constructed from fuel material, body-building material and body-regulating material. No diet is perfect in which these are not all represented. Now, foods are like sections of houses. Some correspond to single parts, as a floor or a window or perhaps a chimney; others to a house complete except for windows and roof; still others to a house lacking only a door or two. It takes some thought to put them together so that we shall have all kinds of parts without a great many extra ones of certain kinds and not enough of others.

Milk is unique in that it comes nearest of all foods to being a complete diet in itself. It is like the house with only a door missing. We could be quite comfortable in such a house for a long time though we could make a more complete diet by adding some graham bread or an apple or some spinach.

We all associate milk with cows and cows with farms, but how closely is milk associated with the farm table? Is it prized as the most valuable food which the farm produces? Every drop should be used as food; and this applies to skim milk, sour milk, and buttermilk as well as sweet milk. Do we all use milk to the best advantage in the diet? Here are a few points which it is well to bear in mind:

Milk will take the place of meat. The world is facing a meat famine. The famine was on the way before the war began but it has approached with tremendous speed this last year. Every cow killed and eaten means not only so much less meat available but so much less of an adequate substitute. Lean meat contributes to the diet chiefly protein and iron. We eat it primarily for the protein. Hence in comparing meat and milk we think first of their protein content. One and one-fourth cups of milk will supply as much protein as two ounces of lean beef. The protein of milk is largely the part which makes cottage cheese. So cottage cheese is a good meat substitute and a practical way of using part of the skim milk when the cream is taken off for butter. One and one-half ounces of cottage cheese (one-fourth cup) are the protein equivalent of two ounces of lean beef. Skim milk and buttermilk are just as good substitutes for meat as whole milk. Since meat is one of the most expensive items in the food bill, its replacement by milk is a very great financial economy. This is true even if the meat is raised on the farm, as food for cattle is used much more economically in the production of milk than of beef.

Milk is the greatest source of calcium (lime). Lime is one of the components of food that serves two purposes; it is both building material for bones and regulating material for the body as a whole, helping in several important ways to maintain good health. It is essential that everyone have a supply of lime and particularly important that all growing infants, children, and young people have plenty for construction of bones and teeth. There is almost none in meat and bread, none in common fats and sugars, and comparatively few common foods can be taken alone and digested in large enough quantities to insure an adequate supply; whereas a pint of milk (whole, skim, or buttermilk) will guarantee to a grown person a sufficient amount, and a quart a day will provide for the greater needs of growing children. Whatever other foods we have, we cannot afford to leave milk out of the diet because of its lime. Under the most favorable dietary conditions, when the diet is liberal and varied, an adult should have *at least* half a pint of milk a day and no child should be expected to thrive with less than a pint.

Milk contains a most varied assortment of materials needed in small amounts for the body welfare, partly for constructive and partly for regulating purposes. These are rather irregularly distributed in other kinds of food materials. When eggs, vegetables, and cereals are freely used, we are not likely to suffer any lack; but when war conditions limit the number of foods which we can get, it is well to remember that the more limited the variety of foods in the diet the more important milk becomes.

Milk will take the place of bread, butter, sugar, and other foods used chiefly for fuel. The body is an engine which must be stoked regularly in order to work. The more work done the more fuel needed. That is what we mean when we talk about the food giving "working strength." A farmer and his wife and usually all the family need much fuel because they do much physical work. Even people whose work is physically light require considerable fuel. A quart of milk will give as much working force as half a pound of bread, one-fourth of a pound of butter, or six ounces of sugar. And this is in addition to the other advantages already mentioned.

Milk contains specifics for growth. Experiments with animals have taught us that there are two specific substances, known as vitamines, which must be present in the diet if a young animal is to grow. If either one is absent, growth is impossible. Both are to be found in milk, one in the cream and the other in the skim milk or whey. For this reason children should have whole milk rather than skim milk. Of course, butter and skim milk should produce the same result as whole milk. Eggs also have these requisites and can be used to supplement milk for either one, but as a rule it is more practical to depend upon milk, and usually more economical.

For little children, milk is best served as a beverage. But as children grow up, the fluidity of milk makes them feel as if it were not food enough and it is generally better to use it freely in the kitchen first, and then, if there is any surplus, put it on the table as a beverage or serve it thus to those who need an extra supply—the half-grown boys, for instance, who need more food in a day than even a hard-working farmer.

A good plan is to set aside definitely, as a day's supply, a quart apiece for each person under sixteen and a pint apiece for each one over this age. Then see at night how well one has succeeded in disposing of it. If there is much left, one should consider ways of using it to advantage. The two simplest probably are, first, as cream sauce for vegetables of all sorts; for macaroni or hominy with or without cheese; or for hard cooked eggs or left-over meats; and next in puddings baked a long time in the oven so that much of the water in the milk is evaporated. Such puddings are easy to prepare on almost any scale and are invaluable for persons with big appetites because they are concentrated without being unwholesome.

The milk pitcher and the vegetable garden are the best friends of the woman wishing to set a wholesome and economical table. Vegetables supplement milk almost ideally, since they contain the vegetable fiber which helps to guard against constipation, and the iron which is the lacking door in the "house that milk built."

Vegetables which are not perfect enough to serve uncooked, like the broken leaves of lettuce and the green and tough parts of celery, are excellent cooked and served with a cream sauce. Cream sauce makes it possible also to cook enough of a vegetable for two days at once, sending it to the table simply dressed in its own juices or a little butter the first time and making a scalloped dish with cream sauce and crumbs the next day. Vegetables which do not lend themselves to this treatment can be made into cream soups, which are excellent as the hot dish for supper, because they can be prepared in the morning and merely reheated at serving time.

Finally, the addition of milk in liberal quantities to tea and coffee (used of course only by adults); its use without dilution with water in cocoa; and instead of water in bread when that is made at home, ought to enable a housewife to dispose satisfactorily of her day's quota of milk. If it should accumulate, it can be dispatched with considerable rapidity in the form of ice cream or milk sherbet. When there is much skim milk, the latter is a most excellent way of making it popular, various fruits in their seasons being used for flavor, as strawberries, raspberries, and peaches, with lemons to fall back on when no native fruit is at hand.

The world needs milk today as badly as wheat. All that we can possibly spare is needed in Europe for starving little ones. In any shortage the slogan must be "children first." But in any limited diet milk is such a safeguard that we should bend our energies to saving it from waste and producing more, rather than learning to do without it. Skim milk from creameries is too valuable to be thrown away. Everyone should be on the alert to condemn any use of milk except as food and to encourage condensation and drying of skim milk to be used as a substitute for fresh milk.

When the milk pitcher is allowed to work its magic for the human race, we shall have citizens of better physique than the records of our recruiting stations show today. Even when the family table is deprived of its familiar wheat bread and meat, we may be strong if we invoke the aid of this friendly magician.

CHAPTER II
CEREALS WE OUGHT TO EAT

(Reprinted from The Farmer's Wife, by permission of the Webb Publishing Company.)

"Save wheat!" This great slogan of our national food campaign has been echoed and reëchoed for six months, but do we yet realize that it means US? We have had, hitherto, a great deal of wheat in our diet. Fully one-third of our calories have come from wheat flour. To ask us to do without wheat is to shake the very foundation of our daily living. How shall we be able to do without it? What shall we substitute for it? These are questions which every housewife must ask and answer before she can take her place in the Amazon Army of Food Conservers.

Is it not strange that out of half a dozen different grains cultivated for human consumption, the demand should concentrate upon wheat? One might almost say that the progress of civilization is marked by raised bread. And wheat has, beyond all other grains, the unique properties that make possible a light, porous yet somewhat tenacious loaf. We like the taste of it, mild but sweet; the feel of it, soft yet firm; the comfort of it, almost perfect digestion of every particle. We have been brought up on it and it is a hardship to change our food habits. It takes courage and resolution. It takes visions of our soldiers crossing the seas to defend us from the greedy eye of militarism and thereby deprived of so many things which we still enjoy. Shall we hold back from them the "staff of life" which they need so much more than we?

Can we live without wheat? Certainly, and live well. We must recognize the scientific fact that no one food (with the exception of milk) is indispensable. There are four letters in the food alphabet: *A*, fuel for the body machine; *B*, protein for the upkeep of the machinery; *C*, mineral salts, partly for upkeep and partly for lubrication—to make all parts work smoothly together; *D*, vitamines, subtle and elusive substances upon whose presence depends the successful use by the body of all the others. These four letters, rightly combined, spell health. They are variously distributed in food materials. Sometimes all are found in one food (milk for example), sometimes only one (as in sugar), sometimes two or three. The amounts also vary in the different foods. To build up a complete diet we have to know how many of these items are present in a given food and also how much of each is there.

Now, cereals are much alike in what they contribute to the diet. In comparing them we are apt to emphasize their differences, much as we do in comparing two men. One man may be a little taller, a little heavier, have a different tilt to his nose, but any two men are more alike than a man and a dog. So corn has a little less protein than wheat and considerably less lime, yet corn and wheat are, nutritionally, more alike than either is like sugar.

None of the cereals will make a complete diet by itself. If we take white bread as the foundation, we must add to it something containing lime, such as milk or cheese; something containing iron, such as spinach, egg yolk, meat, or other iron-rich food; something containing vitamines, such as greens or other vitamine-rich food; something to reënforce the proteins, as milk, eggs, meat, or nuts. It is not possible to make a perfect diet with only one other kind of food besides white bread. It can be done with three: bread, milk, and spinach, for example.

If we substitute whole wheat for white bread, we can make a complete diet with two foods—this and milk. We get from the bran and the germ what in the other case we got from the spinach. *All the cereals can be effectively supplemented by milk and green vegetables.* If green vegetables (or substitutes for them like dried peas and beans or fruit) are hard to get we should give preference to cereals from which the bran coats have not been removed, such as oatmeal and whole wheat. Then the diet will not be deficient in iron, which is not supplied in large enough amounts from white bread and milk. Oatmeal is the richest in iron of all the cereals.

With such knowledge, we may alter our diet very greatly without danger of undernutrition. But we must learn to cook other cereals at least as well as we do wheat. Without proper cooking they are unpalatable and unwholesome, and they are not so easy to cook as wheat. They take a longer time and we cannot get the same culinary effects, since with the exception of rye they will not make a light loaf. Fortunately we are not asked to deny ourselves wheat entirely, only to substitute other cereals for part of it. Let each housewife resolve when next she buys flour to buy at the same time one-fourth as much of some other grain, finely ground, rye, corn, barley, according to preference, and mix the two thoroughly at once. Then she will be sure not to forget to carry out her good intentions. Bread made of such a mixture will be light and tender, and anything that cannot be made with it had better be dispensed with in these times.

Besides the saving of wheat for our country's sake, we shall do well to economize in it for our own. Compared with other cereals, wheat is expensive. We can get more food, in every sense of the word, from half a pound of oatmeal than we can from a twelve-ounce loaf of white bread, and the oatmeal will not cost one-half as much as the bread. A loaf of Boston brown bread made with one cupful each of cornmeal, oatmeal (finely ground), rye flour, molasses, and skim milk will have two and one-half times the food value of a twelve-ounce loaf of white bread and will cost little more. One-half pound of cornmeal, supplemented by a half pint of milk, will furnish more of everything needed by the body than such a twelve-ounce loaf, usually at less cost.

It pays at all times to use cereals in other forms than bread, for both health and economy. Does your family eat cereal for breakfast? A dish of oatmeal made from one-fourth cupful of the dry cereal will take the place of two slices of white bread, each about half an inch thick and three inches square, and give us iron besides. Served with milk, it will make a well-balanced meal. When we add a little fruit to give zest and some crisp corn bread to contrast with the soft mush, we have a meal in which we may take a just pride, *provided the oatmeal is properly cooked.*

A good dish of oatmeal is as creditable a product as a good loaf of bread. It cannot be made without taking pains to get the right proportions of meal, water, and salt, and to cook thoroughly, which means at least four hours in a double boiler, over night in a fireless cooker, or half an hour at twenty pounds in a pressure cooker. Half-cooked oatmeal is most unwholesome, as well as unpalatable. It is part of our patriotic duty not to give so useful a food a bad reputation.

The man who does hard physical labor, especially in the open air, may complain that the oatmeal breakfast does not "stay by" him. This is because it digests rapidly. What he needs is a little fat stirred into the mush before it is sent to the table, or butter as well as milk and sugar served with it. If one must economize, the cereal breakfast should always be the rule. It is impossible in any other way to provide for a family adequately on a small sum, especially where there are growing children.

Next to oatmeal, hominy is one of the cheapest breakfast foods. It has less flavor and is improved by the addition of a few dates cut into quarters or some small stewed seedless raisins, which also add the iron which hominy lacks. For the adults of the family the staying qualities of hominy and cornmeal can be increased by cutting the molded mush in slices and frying till a crisp crust is formed. This can be obtained more easily if the cereals are cooked in a mixture of milk and water instead of water alone. The milk supplements the cereal as acceptably as in a dish of mush and milk. Cornmeal needs even more cooking than oatmeal to develop an agreeable flavor. It can be improved by the addition of an equal amount of farina or cream of wheat.

Cereals for dinner are acceptable substitutes for such vegetables as potatoes, both for economy and for variety. The whole grains, rice, barley, and hominy, lend themselves best to such use. Try a dish of creamed salmon with a border of barley; one of hominy surrounded by fried apples; or a bowl of rice heaped with bananas baked to a turn and removed from their skins just before serving, and be glad that the war has stirred you out of food ruts!

Cereals combined with milk make most wholesome puddings, each almost a well-balanced meal in itself. They are easier to make than pies, shortcakes, and other desserts which require wheat flour, and they are splendid growing food for boys and girls.

For the hard-working man who misses the slowly-digesting pie, serve the puddings with a hard sauce or add a little butter when making them. For the growing children, raisins, dates, and other fruits are welcome additions on account of their iron. From half a cupful to a cupful of almost any cereal pudding made with milk is the equivalent of an ordinary serving of pie.

Aside from the avoidance of actual waste of food materials, there seems to be no one service so imperative for housewives to render in these critical times as the mastery of the art of using cereals. These must be made to save not only wheat but meat, and for most of us also money.

A wholesome and yet economical diet may be built upon a plan wherein we find for an average working man fourteen ounces of cereal food and one pint of milk, from two to four ounces of meat or a good meat substitute, two ounces of fat, three ounces of sugar or other sweeteners, at least one kind of fruit, and one kind of vegetable besides potatoes (more if one has a garden).

The cereal may furnish half the fuel value of the diet, partly bread-stuffs and partly in some of the other ways as suggested, without any danger of undernutrition. Remember the fable of the farmer who told his sons he had left them a fortune and bade them dig on his farm for it after his death, and how they found wealth not as buried treasure but through thorough tillage of the soil. So one might leave a message to woman to look in the cereal pot, for there is a key to health and wealth, and a weapon to win the greatest war the world has ever seen.

CHAPTER III
THE MEAT WE OUGHT TO SAVE

"Do not buy a pound of meat until you have bought three quarts of milk" is a "war sign" pointing two ways. On the one hand it tells us that we need to save meat; on the other, that we should encourage the production of that most indispensable food—milk.

But what a revolution in some households if this advice is heeded! Statisticians tell us that Americans have been consuming meat at the rate of 171 pounds per capita per year, which means nearly half a pound apiece every day for each man, woman, child, and infant in arms. Now, as mere infants and some older folk have not had any, it follows that many of us have had a great deal more. Did we need it? Shall we be worse off without it? Meat is undeniably popular. In spite of the rising price and the patriotic spirit of conservation, meat consumption goes on in many quarters at much the usual rate. There is probably no other one food so generally liked. It has a decided and agreeable flavor, a satisfactory "chew," and leaves an after-sense of being well fed that many take as the sign of whether they are well nourished or not. It digests well, even when eaten rapidly, and perhaps partly for this reason is favored by the hurried man of affairs. It is easy to prepare and hence is appreciated by the cook, who knows that even with unskillful treatment it will be acceptable and require few accessories to make an agreeable meal. Its rich flavor helps to relieve the flatness of foods like rice, hominy, beans, or bread. From this point of view there is no such thing as a "meat substitute."

But, nutritionally speaking, meat is only one of many; undeniably a good source of protein, but no better than milk or eggs. A lamb chop is a very nice item on a bill of fare, but the protein it contains can be secured just as well from one large egg, or two level tablespoonfuls of peanut butter, or one and one-fourth ounces of cheese; or a part of the time from a quarter of a cup of dried navy beans or a little less of dried split peas.

Meat is highly regarded as a source of iron; but, again, it has no monopoly of this important building-stone in the house of diet. The eggs, or peas, or half the beans mentioned above would any one of them furnish more iron than the lamb chop, while a quarter of a cup of cooked spinach or a small dish of string beans would furnish quite as much. Besides green vegetables, fruit, and the yolk of egg, cereals are a not inconsiderable source of iron. A man would have adequate nourishment for a day, including a sufficient supply of iron, if he were doing only moderate physical labor, from one pint of milk, one and one-half pounds of whole wheat bread, and three medium-sized apples. Beef juice is often used as a source of iron for children and undoubtedly it is one which is palatable and digestible, but it takes a quarter of a pound of beef to get a few tablespoonfuls of juice, and a tablespoonful of juice would hardly contain as much iron as one egg yolk; and it seems probable that the iron of the egg yolk would be better utilized for the making of good red blood.

Meat is good fuel for the human machine if used in moderate amounts along with other food. But meat is no better fuel than other food. An ordinary lamb chop will furnish no more calories than a dish of oatmeal, a piece of bread an inch thick and three inches square, a large apple or banana, an egg, five ounces (five-eighths of a cup) of milk, or a tablespoonful of peanut butter. The fatter meat is the higher its fuel value (providing the fat is used for food). A tablespoonful of bacon fat or beef drippings has the same fuel value as a tablespoonful of butter or lard, or as the lamb chop mentioned above. The man who insists that he has to have meat for working strength judges by how he feels after a meal and not by the scientific facts. While in the long run appetite serves as a measure of food requirement, we can find plenty of instances where it does not make a perfect measure. Some people have too large appetites for their body needs and get too fat from sheer surplus of fuel stored in the body for future needs as fat. If such people have three good meals a day all the time, there never is any future need and the fat stays. Other people have too small appetites for their needs and they never seem to get a surplus of fuel on hand. They live, as it were, from hand to mouth. Anyone accustomed to eating meat will have an unsatisfied feeling at first after a meal without meat. The same is true of other highly flavored foods. It is well for the cook to bear this in mind and serve a few rather highly seasoned dishes when there is no meat on the bill of fare. A very sweet dessert will often satisfy this peculiar sensation, and it can be allayed, at least in part, by the drinking of water some little time after the meal. Such a sensation will pass away when one becomes accustomed to the change in diet. It is probably due to certain highly flavored substances dissolved in the meat juices which are known to be excellent stimulants to the flow of gastric juice and which are stimulating in other ways. These have no food value in themselves, but, nevertheless, we prize meat for them, as is shown by the distaste we have for meat which has its juices removed. "Soup meat" has always been a problem for the housewife—hard to make palatable—and yet the greater part of the nourishment of meat is left in the meat itself after soup is made from it.

Let us frankly recognize then that we eat meat because we like it—for its flavor and texture rather than any peculiar nourishing properties—and that it is only our patriotic self-denial or force of economic circumstances that induces us to forgo our accustomed amounts of a food which is pleasant and (in moderation) wholesome. We must save meat that the babies of the world may have milk to drink. Nowhere in Europe is there enough milk for babies today. A conservative request for one European city alone was a shipment of one million pounds of condensed milk per month! If cattle are killed for food there will be little milk to send and the babies will perish. We must save meat for our soldiers and sailors, because they need it more than we do. It is not only easily transported, but one of the few things to give zest to their necessarily limited fare. Fresh fruits and green vegetables, which may serve us as appetizers, are not to be found on the war fields. Dainty concoctions from cheese and nuts may provide for us flavor as well as nutriment, but meat is the alternative to the dull monotony of bread and beans for the soldier—the tonic of appetite, the stimulant to good digestion. We can scarcely send him anything to take its place.

We must save meat, too, as a general food economy. Meat is produced at the expense of grain, which we might eat ourselves. And the production of meat is a very wasteful process. Grains have a fuel value for man approximating 1,600 calories per pound. A pound of meat in the form of beef will require the consumption by the animal of some fourteen pounds of grain. The pound of beef will furnish perhaps 1,200 calories, while the grain consumed will represent over 20,000 calories. The production of milk from grain is only about one-third as expensive, so the purchase of three quarts of milk to one pound of meat is an economy in more ways than one.

Saving for the rest of the world will not be without some physical advantage to ourselves, if we have been accustomed to indulge in meat freely. Among the well-to-do meat eating is apt to be overdone to the extent of affecting the kidneys and the arteries, and some enforced restriction would be a real advantage to health, as has been demonstrated in other than war times. Because a food is good is no reason for unlimited quantities; an ounce of sugar a day is wholesome—a pound is likely to result in both indigestion and a badly balanced diet. A quarter of a pound of meat a day is not undesirable for an adult, but a pound a day may result in general overeating or in the special ills which are related directly to a large quantity of meat. One of these is an upsetting of a proper balance of food elements in the diet. Diets high in meat are apt to be low in milk and consequently low in calcium. If the income is limited this is almost sure to be the case, since there will not be enough money to provide meat freely and at the same time satisfy other nutritive requirements. Such diets are also likely to be low in fuel value and not provide enough working force even while men are declaring that they must have meat to give them strength. They would have more strength and a better diet from every point of view if part of the meat money were spent for milk. So the injunction to buy three quarts of milk to one pound of meat is a good rule for securing a well balanced and ample diet at the lowest cost.

Another good rule is to spend no more for meat, fish, and eggs than for milk, and as much for fruits and vegetables as for meat, fish, and eggs. Families very commonly spend as much as one-third of the food money for meat; and, while they may secure a full third of their protein, iron, and phosphorus in this way, they may not get more than a sixth of their fuel and almost no calcium. Three quarts of milk at fourteen cents a quart will yield about 2,000 calories. For an expenditure of forty-two cents for beef as free from waste as milk, we would pay perhaps thirty-two cents per pound. A pound and a quarter of lean beef would yield about 1,000 calories. So as fuel alone the milk would be twice as cheap as the meat. Three quarts of milk would yield almost if not quite as much protein as the meat and a liberal supply of calcium to offset the iron furnished by the meat. Everything considered, then, milk is a better investment than meat. The same is true of some of the other foods which supply protein in the diet such as dry peas and beans; cheese and peanut butter are at least twice as valuable nutritionally as beef. The domestic problem is to make palatable dishes from these foods. This requires time and patience. The cook must not get discouraged if the first trial does not bring marked success. The rest of the family should count it their "bit" to eat valiantly until they can eat joyfully.

CHAPTER IV

THE POTATO AND ITS SUBSTITUTES

Never did it seem truer that "blessings brighten as they take their flight" than when the potato went off the market or soaring prices put it out of reach in the winter of 1917. "How shall I plan my meals without it?" was the housewife's cry. "How shall I enjoy my meals without it?" said all the millions of potato eaters who immediately forgot that there was still a large number of foods from which they might extract some modicum of enjoyment.

And so the Nutrition Expert was asked to talk about "potato substitutes" and expected to exercise some necromancy whereby that which was not a potato might become a potato. Now, the Nutrition Expert was very imperturbable—not at all disturbed by the calamity which had befallen our tables. That unfeeling person saw potatoes, not in terms of their hot mealiness and spicy mildness, but in terms of that elusive thing called "DIET." The vanishing tuber was bidden to answer the dietary roll-call:

"Proteins?"	"Here!"	Answer somewhat faint but suggesting remarkable worth.
"Fats?"	No answer.	
"Carbohydrates?"	Loud note from	"Starch."
"Mineral salts?"	"Here!"	From a regular chorus, among which "Potassium" and "Iron" easily distinguishable.
"Vitamines and Other Accessories?"	"Here! Here!"	Especially vociferous, the "Anti-Scorbutic Property."

"This is a good showing for any single food material. The potato, as truly as bread, may be called a 'staff of life.' Men have lived in health upon it for many months without any other food save oleomargarine. Its protein, though small in amount, is most efficient in body-building, its salts are varied in kind and liberal in amount, and it furnishes a large amount of very easily digested fuel besides. It is at its best when cooked in the simplest possible way—baked or boiled in its skin. Nevertheless we are not absolutely dependent upon the potato."

"Alas," said the housewife, "this doesn't tell me what to cook for dinner!"

"Patience, Madam, we shall see about that." The fact that starch is present is what makes the potato seem so substantial. But bread, rice, hominy, in fact, all cereal foods can supply starch just as well. Pick out the one you fancy and serve it for your dinner. One good-sized roll or a two-inch cube of corn bread, or three-fourths of a cup of boiled rice will sustain you just as well as a medium-sized potato. A banana, baked or fried, makes an excellent substitute for a potato. An apple is also a very palatable potato equivalent, if you want something more spicy than hominy or corn bread. Why mourn over the lost potato?

But how about those mineral salts? Well, the potato has no monopoly on those, either, though it is ordinarily a very valuable contributor. Milk has already been mentioned as one of the great safeguarding sources of so-called ash constituents. Others are vegetables and fruits of different kinds. These have been a neglected and sometimes a despised part of the diet: "Why spend money for that which is not meat?" is often taken literally. Even food specialists have been known to say, "Fruits and vegetables are mostly water and indigestible fiber; they have little food value." This is a good deal like saying, "If your coat be long enough you do not need a pair of shoes." A potato has as much iron as an egg yolk or a medium-sized chop. This is one more reason why we should be sorry to take the useful tuber from our tables, but we may feel a certain independence, even when meat and eggs are prohibitive in price, since by canning or drying, if in no other way, we can have green vegetables as a source of iron the whole year through. Some people are afraid that canned vegetables will prove unwholesome; but if removed from the can as soon as opened and heated to boiling before they are eaten, we are recently assured that the danger of food poisoning will be materially lessened. Even when such vegetables are wanted for salads, boiling and subsequent cooling are advised. The mineral salts of vegetables dissolve into the water in which they stand, and in any shortage of such food, or for the greatest economy, it would seem wise to save the water in the can, which is often thrown away to secure a more delicate flavor. Water from the cooking of fresh vegetables which are not protected by skins (among them spinach, peas, carrots, and asparagus), can often be reduced to a small amount by steaming instead of boiling the vegetable, or any drained off can be used in gravy, soup, sauce, or some similar fashion. The strong flavor of some vegetables, however, makes such economy rather impractical.

Some people discriminate against canned and dried vegetables because they do not taste like fresh ones. This seems rather unreasonable, as we want a variety of flavors in our diet and might welcome the change which comes from this way of treating food as well as that which comes from different methods of cooking. Nobody expects a stew to taste like a roast, and yet both may be good and we would not want either one all the time. Instead of regretting that canned peas do not taste like those fresh from the garden (incomparable ones!) let us be glad that they taste as good as they do. Would we like them any better if they tasted like cornmeal mush?

While a potato has about as much phosphorus as an egg yolk, substitutes for it in this respect are not hard to find. Five tablespoonfuls of milk or half an ounce of cheese will easily supply as much, while half a cup of cooked string beans will provide all the iron as well as half the phosphorus in a potato, and a teaspoon of butter or other fat added to the beans will make them equal in fuel value. On the other hand, two small slices of whole wheat bread would furnish all the phosphorus, half the iron, and an equal amount of fuel.

The potato is conspicuously high in potassium, but it is not likely that in any diet containing one kind of fruit and one kind of vegetable each day there will be any permanent shortage of this substance. Spinach, celery, parsnips, lettuce, cabbage, rutabagas, beets, carrots, tomatoes, cucumbers, and turnips are all good sources of potassium and some of them are available all the year round without canning and drying.

But what significance has the "Anti-Scorbutic Property"? Does that not make potatoes indispensable? Scurvy, Madam, occurs whenever people live for a long time on a monotonous diet without fresh food. The potato offers good protection against this disease at a low cost, but other foods have long been known to possess the same power, among them oranges, lemons, limes, and other fruits, and cabbage and other green vegetables; in fact, a mixed diet in which fruits and vegetables occur is assurance of freedom from scurvy. Just how far the potato will go in providing the specific vitamines essential for growth is still unsettled. It undoubtedly contains one of them in goodly amount, but for the present it is wise to include some green (leaf) vegetable in the diet even when potatoes are plentiful, especially if butter, milk, and eggs cannot be freely used.

Nutritionally then, we can find substitutes for the potato; practically, too, we can find quite satisfactory alternatives for it in our conventional bills of fare. On the face of things the potato is a bland mealy food which blends well with the high flavor and the firm texture of meat and the softness of many other cooked vegetables. Gastronomically, rice or hominy comes about as near to having the same qualities, with hot bread, macaroni, sweet potatoes, and baked bananas (underripe so as not to be too juicy and sweet) close rivals. These are not so easy to cook and serve as the potato and are not likely to supplant it when it is plentiful. It might be worth while, however, to substitute these for potatoes rather often. The latter will be appreciated all the more if not served every day in the week, or at least not more than once a day. We might extend the fashion of baked beans and brown bread to roast pork with rice, ham with baked bananas, roast beef with hominy, and broiled steak with macaroni. Why not? You, Madam Housewife, are always sighing for variety, but does it never occur to you that the greatest secret of variety lies in new combinations?

CHAPTER V

ARE FRUITS AND VEGETABLES LUXURIES?

In the house of diet fruits and vegetables may be likened to windows and doors, fire-places and chimneys; we could dispense with them, we could board up our windows and make a fire on a big stone in the middle of the room, letting the smoke escape through a hole in the roof, but such a course would not mean comfort year in and year out. So we may exist without fruits and vegetables, but it is worth while to stop and consider what we gain by their use.

We shall have to admit at the outset that if we have to spend money or labor for them, fruits and vegetables are not the cheapest source of fuel for the human machine. Some of them are cheaper fuel than butter, eggs, or meat, but not as cheap as cereals, sugar, molasses, syrups, and some of our cheapest fats. This is true of potatoes, parsnips, carrots, dried peas and beans, and such fruits as bananas, prunes, raisins, dates, figs, and possibly a few other dried fruits, but we cannot justify our investment in most fruits and vegetables solely on the plea that they are "filling" in the sense of being of high fuel value; on this ground lettuce, celery, cabbage, tomatoes, lemons, rhubarb, cranberries, and many others would find no place in our domestic economy.

Remembering that man does not live by fuel alone, we may find ample reasons for spending some of our food money upon things which at first thought seem to give an inadequate return. There is an old adage, "An apple a day keeps the doctor away," which if true means that the apple is a real economy, a kind of health insurance, for an apple costs seldom over five cents—often only one—and a doctor's visit may easily cost a hundred times as much. There is a certain amount of truth in the saying, though the apple does not have a monopoly of the supposed virtue. It is more accurate, if less poetic, to say that an *assortment* of fruits and vegetables helps to keep us in good health. Before the days of modern "cold pack" canning, mothers used to assemble their little home groups in the spring and, in spite of sundry hidings under tables on the part of reluctant Johnnies and Susies, dutifully portion out herb tea or sulphur in molasses. Spring cleaning could never stop short of "cleansing the blood!" And after a monotonous winter of salt pork and fried potatoes no doubt heroic measures were necessary to make up for an ill-chosen diet. Nowadays we recognize no such seasonal need. We carry our surplus of fruits and vegetables over from summer to winter and profit not only in the greater daily pleasure of our tables but in clearer skins, brighter eyes, and less "spring fever."

How do fruits and vegetables help to keep us well? In the first place, by their wholesome effect upon the bowels. As a rule we associate regular daily movements with health, but do not always recognize the part which diet plays in securing them. If we eat little besides meat and potatoes, bread, butter, and cake or pie, we are very likely to have constipation. This is particularly true for those who work indoors or sit much of the time. Now, fruits and vegetables have several properties which help to make them laxative. Many have considerable woody fiber. In celery and asparagus we find it in actual "strings"; in cabbage, spinach, lettuce, and other stem or leaf vegetables it may not be so noticeable, but it is certainly present and we should realize that it is useful. The skins of fruit are of this nature and may often be eaten, as in case of prunes, figs, apples, dried peaches and apricots. The outer coats of grains, which serve the same purpose, are frequently removed by milling, but similar coats of peas and beans are not so removed except in the case of dried split peas. In the juices of fruits and vegetables we find a variety of laxative substances. This explains why apple juice (sweet cider), orange juice or diluted lemon juice may be a very desirable morning drink. The effect is partly due to the acid but not wholly. Juices which are not acid to the taste, as those of prunes, figs, onions, have laxative properties. So from a great variety of fruits and vegetables, especially those which are fibrous or acid or both, we may obtain the substitute for "pills" in wholesome foods which are generally cheaper than drugs.

No diet can be properly built without a suitable supply of mineral salts. The free use of milk is our greatest safeguard against lack of any save iron, but when milk is scarce and has to be saved as now for the babies of the world, it is fortunate that we can make fruits and vegetables take its place in part. Some of our very common vegetables are good sources of the calcium (lime) and phosphorus so freely supplied in milk. Among these may be taken as an example the carrot, which has not had due recognition in many quarters and in some is even spoken of contemptuously as "cattle food." Its cheapness comes from the fact that it is easy to grow and easy to keep through the winter and should not blind us to its merits. A good-sized carrot (weight one-fourth pound) will have only about half the fuel value of a medium-sized potato, but nearly ten times as much calcium as the potato and about one-third more phosphorus. While actual figures show that other vegetables, especially parsnips, turnips, celery, cauliflower, and lettuce, are richer in calcium than the carrot, its cheapness and fuel value make it worthy of emphasis. Everyone who has a garden should devote some space to this pretty and palatable vegetable. It is perhaps at its best when steamed till soft without salting and then cut up into a nicely seasoned white sauce; its sweetness will not then be destroyed nor its salts lost in the cooking water. It is not only useful as a hot vegetable, but in salads, in the form of a toothsome marmalade, and as the foundation of a steamed pudding. For little children it is most wholesome and they should make its acquaintance by the time they are a year and a half old, in the form of a cream soup. A dish of carrots and peas (one-half cup peas, one-fourth cup carrot cubes, one-half cup white sauce) will have almost the same food values (for fuel, calcium, phosphorus, and iron) as an equivalent serving of oatmeal, milk, and sugar (three-fourths cup cooked oatmeal, one-half cup milk, one rounding teaspoon sugar) and will add variety to the diet without costing a great deal more unless one pays a fancy price for peas.

Even when meat and eggs are not prohibitive in price, fruit and green vegetables are an important source of iron in the diet. And when war conditions make the free consumption of meat unpatriotic, it is reassuring to think that we really can get along without meat very well if we know how. Two ounces of lean beef will furnish no more iron than a quarter of a cup of cooked spinach or half a cup of cooked string beans or dried beans, or one-sixth of a cup of raisins, or half a dozen good-sized prunes. Cabbage, peas, lettuce, dandelion greens, beet tops, turnip tops and other "greens" are well worth including in our bill of fare for their iron alone. By the time children are a year old we begin to introduce special iron-bearing foods into their diet to supplement milk. Aside from egg yolk, we give preference for this purpose to green vegetable juice or pulp, especially from peas and spinach or a mixture of both. The substantial character of dry beans is too well known to require comment, but how many realize that they are a most valuable source of iron and other mineral salts? The fact that they are not a "complete diet" in themselves should not disturb anyone who realizes that all diets are built from a variety of foods. We are hardly likely to use beans to the exclusion of everything else except in dire necessity, and then what better could we do than use freely a food which will go so far toward sustaining life at so small a cost?

There is a further significance for fruits and vegetables in their contribution to the diet of the growth-promoting, health-protecting vitamines. That the presence of fruits and vegetables in the diet is a safeguard against scurvy is well known, though the full scientific explanation is not yet ours. That the leaf vegetables (spinach, lettuce, cabbage, and the like) contain both the vitamines which are essential to growth in the young and to the maintenance of health in the adult seems assured, and gives us further justification for emphasis on green vegetables in the diet of little children, when properly administered—i.e., always cooked, put through a fine sieve, and fed in small quantities.

Aside from being valuable for regulation of the bowels, for mineral salts, and vitamines, to say nothing of more or less fuel value, fruits and vegetables give zest to the diet. The pleasant acidity of many fruits, their delicate aroma, their beautiful form and coloring, the ease of preparing them for the table, are qualities for which we may legitimately prize them, though we may not spend money for them until actual nutritive requirements are met. Dr. Simon Patten, in his *New Basis for Civilisation*, ably expresses the value of appetizers: "Tomatoes, the hothouse delicacy of the Civil War time, are doing now what many a bloody revolution failed to accomplish; they have relieved the monotony of the salt pork and boiled potatoes upon the poor man's table. The clear acid flavor of the canned vegetable lightens ugly heaviness and adds tonic gratifications for the lack of which men have let each other's blood."

As already remarked, those who have plenty of highly flavored meat are apt to be satisfied by it or to demand stronger flavors (coffee, catsup, pickles, and tobacco) than those found in fruits and vegetables. They are also apt to spend so much money on meat that they have none left to buy what seem to them unimportant items in the diet, and to have a much less wholesome diet than they might have for the same money. Studies of expenditures in many families show that a good rule to insure a well balanced diet is to spend no more money for meat than one does for fruit and vegetables. Also, it is well to remember that vegetables are usually cheaper than fruits and that dried ones may largely take the place of canned or fresh ones. For wholesome and economical living, have fruit of some kind at least once a day and make the main dish of one meal a vegetable dish whenever possible. Thick cream soups, souffles, creamed or scalloped vegetables, are all substantial and appetizing. The way to learn to like such foods is to keep trying. One may learn contentment with the proverbial dinner of herbs more easily by realizing that one is building valuable bricks into the house of diet; and in the present emergency one may, by selection of fruits and vegetables of high energy value, save less perishable foods for our soldiers and allies. The knowledge that a banana is equivalent in calories to a large slice of bread or a small pat of butter becomes tremendously significant; that an apple, an orange, four prunes, four dates, or a cup of peas, may not only take the place of bread but actually add something which the bread does not contain, means that we may be the gainers from our own sacrifices, without embarrassment thereat. We shall have reaped a speedy reward for doing our duty.

CHAPTER VI

FATS AND VITAMINES

In the days of the ancient Romans vegetable oils were prized for food and butter was used for cosmetics. In America today we are asking what is to become of us if we cannot have butter to eat! Such are the fashions in food. "June butter" is one of our gastronomic traditions. The sample in the restaurant may have none of the firm creamy texture and delicate aromatic flavor of the product of the old spring house; but as long as it is labeled butter we try to bring our sensations into line with our imaginations. For the real butter flavor there is no more a substitute than there is for the aroma of coffee. But these are matters of esthetic pleasure rather than of nutrition. They depend largely upon habit. Whale blubber and seal oil are as much appreciated in some quarters as butter is by us. An American going inland from the Atlantic coast is often surprised to find that olive oil, instead, of being served on every table, is exceedingly disliked.

For the sustenance of the body we must recognize that fat is fat, whatever its flavor. A calorie from butter yields neither more nor less energy than a calorie from lard or bacon, olive oil or cottonseed oil. The common food fats are all very well digested if judiciously used—not in too large quantities, nor over-heated in cooking, and not "cooked into" things too much as in pastries, rich sauces, and fried foods. Whether we spread our bread with butter or beef drippings amounts to the same thing in the long run; the main point is which we are willing to eat.

A change is rapidly coming over our food habits. The price of butter has been soaring beyond our reach, and the market for "butterine," "nut margarine," "oleomargarine," or whatever the substitute table fat may be called, has expanded tremendously. It is excellent household economy to buy milk and a butter substitute rather than cream or butter. In these substitutes refined vegetable oils such as cottonseed, cocoanut, and peanut, and oils derived from beef or lard are so combined or treated as to produce the desired hardness, and churned with milk or milk and butter to improve texture and flavor. Lard substitutes are similarly made from one or more of these fats, but are harder in texture and no attempt is made to give them a butter flavor by churning with milk. All the fats used are wholesome and efficient sources of energy for the human machine.

In the absence of butter some other form of fat is desirable in the diet, because fat is so concentrated a food. There is a limit to the capacity of the human stomach to hold food. People who live on a diet largely of rice, which has almost no fat in its make-up, develop characteristically distended abdomens, because they have to eat such a great quantity of food to get fuel enough for their day's work. When people are for any reason put on a milk diet for a considerable time it is customary to put something into the milk to make it more concentrated, for otherwise they would drink and drink and then hardly get fuel enough. To give a concrete illustration—a man's energy requirement for a day may be met by from four to five quarts of milk (unless he is doing very heavy manual labor), but it would be much more practical to substitute a loaf of bread, which is comparatively dry, for one quart of milk, and three ounces of fat (six tablespoonfuls) for another quart of milk, making the total volume but little over half what it would be if four quarts of milk were taken. For people who are engaged in hard physical toil, fat is exceedingly important for this purpose of gaining in concentration. "Fat is fuel for fighters," and it is perfectly reasonable to ask those who are not doing much heavy labor to eat other kinds of food and save fat for those who simply have to have it to do their work well. In the ordinary mixed diet one can easily dispense with an ounce of fat (two tablespoonfuls). Each tablespoonful is equalled in energy by an apple, or a banana, a large egg, two half-inch slices of bread about three inches square, four dates, four prunes—and it is no great strain on one's capacity for food to substitute such items for the fat.

On account of its concentration, fat is good for transportation; and aside from its energy value it gives the diet "staying" qualities. Other things being equal, one feels hungry sooner after a meal without fat than after one in which it is liberally supplied. People doing manual labor, and especially out of doors, feel the pangs of hunger more than sedentary folks and hence need more fat to keep them comfortable. No man can do his best work when all the time thinking how hungry he is. It behooves us all then, as good citizens, to recognize the greater need of our soldiers and sailors and our hard-working laborers for as liberal allowances of fat as we can make. At the same time, we cannot for our own best health dispense with fat altogether. We may consider anything up to two ounces apiece a day legitimate for our own maintenance of efficiency.

In departing from food customs there is a natural timidity lest the new food shall in some way be less healthful than the old. Recent scientific researches have revealed a hitherto unsuspected property in butter, a discovery which has aroused some concern as to whether we can safely substitute other fats for it. Young animals fed on a diet of highly purified food materials in which lard is the only kind of fat may seem fairly well but do not grow normally, while those fed the same diet in every respect except that the lard is replaced by butter grow as young animals should and are more resistant to disease. Study of other food fats shows that they may be divided into two groups, one with this growth promoting property and one without it. In general, the vegetable oils do not have it, while butter and beef oil do; on the other hand, lard does not have it, while the oil from corn does. Careful analysis of the situation has shown that a fat-soluble vitamine is present which can in the laboratory be separated from the fat. This same vitamine is present in a variety of food materials—in whole milk, in egg yolks, in leaves of plants—but we have not studied it long enough to know just how much spinach we can substitute for a tablespoonful of butter so far as the vitamine is concerned. We must await further investigations. But we may rest assured that with a fairly liberal amount of milk and some green vegetables, possibly some beef fat, we need not fear any disastrous consequences from the substitution of some other fat for butter. Where the diet is limited and the entire quantity of fat is not very large, it seems prudent to select oleomargarine made largely from beef oil and, where circumstances permit its use without the sacrifice of any other dietary essential, to use butter in the diet of growing children unless they get a full quart of milk apiece a day.

Changing our food customs is difficult because it means also changing our cooking customs. But many dishes can be made with less fat than we are accustomed to put in or with different kinds from those we have hitherto preferred. Often the fat from frying is left in the pan to be washed out and thrown away. If every cook could say to herself, "Every two drops of fat make a calorie and every calorie counts in the world today," it might seem more worth while to hold the pan a minute and drain out the fat for further use. A thousand calories mean a day's life to a baby. It is always more wholesome to cook foods so that they are not coated with fat, and one may get brown products in a frying pan without more than a thin film of fat to keep the food from sticking. It is well to remember in this connection that the unsalted lard substitutes are more satisfactory than the saltier fat foods, in which there may be a trace of milk.

The thought that fat is fuel wherever we find it in food will stiffen our resolution to take a little pains with the fats which we have been wont to discard. Anyone can get from the Department of Agriculture suggestions for the practical use of chicken, mutton, beef, and other kinds of meat fats. The main points are to free them from flavor, by melting them with milk or water, possibly using some special absorbent like potato or charcoal too, and then mixing hard and soft together, just as the oleomargarine-makers do, to get such a degree of hardness as suits one's purpose. All this requires time and thought. Let no one dream that the patriotic duties of the kitchen are trivial. Anything that is worth while costs something; money, thought, labor—perhaps all three. To salvage kitchen fat may not be economical in time and labor (though it generally is more so than one might think), but there is more time and labor than food available today. So it seems the "bit" of the housekeeper to set a standard for her family as to the amount of fat she will purchase per week, which is at least one-fourth lower than their ordinary consumption, and to depend upon special conservation of what may have gone to waste hitherto for any increase in this allowance.

CHAPTER VII
"SUGAR AND SPICE AND EVERYTHING NICE"

"Do come and taste how nice the burnt pig eats!" So cried the miscreant son of Hati when his attempt to rescue his father's live-stock from utter destruction resulted (at least according to Lamb) in adding one more delicacy to the table of civilized man. That the "burnt pig" commended itself instantly to the taste of other men is attested by the recklessness with which they ignited their own houses to secure the new sensation again.

Not all flavors make an immediate appeal. Many persons can mark the time when they learned to like olives, or tomatoes, or tea. The taste for some foods was acquired so early that there is no consciousness of any time when they were not enjoyed, and the impression prevails that the liking for such foods is instinctive. Sometimes that is the case, but quite as often not. Children have to be taught by patient repetition to like most of the common foods which make the staples of the diet, and likings thus acquired are as strong as those which seem more natural.

However taste be accounted for, we have to recognize the fact that food is chosen for flavor more than for ultimate benefit. It is one thing to say that oatmeal is more nutritious than bread and coffee; it is quite another to induce a man to give up the latter for the former! And yet the distinguishing characteristic of man is that he can subjugate his immediate impulses for his future benefit, or find a course that will harmonize the two—take coffee with his oatmeal for instance, or find some way to flavor it, perhaps with sugar.

Probably no one flavor is so universally enjoyed as sweetness. "Sweeter than the honey in the honey comb" is an ancient symbol of appreciation. When the sugar bowl is empty how many things lose zest! Tea, coffee, cocoa, breakfast cereals, fruit, might still be acceptable, but cake, pie, and ice cream are unthinkable without sweetness; the soda fountain, the bakery, and the candy shop bear further testimony to our love of sweets. Four million tons of sugar a year for the American people—eighty-five pounds apiece, nearly a quarter of a pound apiece daily—this is no inconsiderable amount of flavoring!

But is not sugar good food? Most assuredly. Three lumps of sugar would furnish the extra energy needed to walk a mile; a quarter of a pound represents about one-sixth of a man's daily fuel requirement. But one baked potato would furnish the same energy as the three lumps of sugar; a quarter of a pound of cornstarch would supply the same fuel as the quarter pound of sugar. Nutritionally starch and sugar are interchangeable, the advantage as far as digestion is concerned being with the starch rather than the sugar. And yet we put sugar on starch! So much for instinct being a guide to scientific food combinations!

The problem of doing without sugar is primarily a problem of flavor—a problem of finding something else which is sweet. Hence we turn our cornstarch into glucose (make corn syrup, for example) outside the body instead of inside it, so that we can taste the sweetness as it goes down. The main trouble with this kind of sugar is that it is not sweet enough to satisfy us and we are apt to use too much, thus endangering our digestions by sheer concentration of what would be, in smaller quantities, most wholesome. Once more we see that nutrition is largely a question of *how much*; how much glucose or other sugar our stomachs can stand we find out by experience; few stomachs can stand when empty the quantity represented by a lollipop, and yet we frequently see children allowed to suck these between meals. The same amount of sugar diluted with water, as in a glass of lemonade, would do less harm; it might be combined with flour in a cooky with more impunity; better yet, it might be made a part of a whole meal, taking it in several dishes (sauce, dessert, etc.), or, if we must have it as candy, at the end of the meal. Used in this way, the advantages of sugar as a food may be had with relatively little disadvantage.

Honey, "the distilled sweetness of the flower," commands a price commensurate with the exquisiteness of its production, but is not quite as easy of digestion as some other forms of sugar. Because of its intense sweetness it may be combined with advantage with less sweet syrups, such as corn syrup. The cook estimates that by measure it will take one and a half times as much corn syrup as cane sugar to get the customary effects in sweet dishes. By using one part of honey to three of corn syrup a sweeter product is obtained, which is free from several of the disadvantages of honey in cookery.

Maple syrup and sugar are not only prized for their sweetness, due to the presence of ordinary cane sugar, but for the delicate "maple" flavor so difficult to duplicate. Nutritionally a tablespoon of maple sugar is equivalent in fuel value to about four-fifths of a tablespoon of cane sugar, while equal volumes of cane molasses, corn syrup, and maple syrup are interchangeable as fuel, though not of equal sweetening power.

Molasses is a less one-sided food than cane sugar or corn syrup. The latter furnish nothing but fuel, and if used too freely not only disturb digestion but tend to crowd out foods which yield mineral salts. Molasses is quite rich in calcium, one tablespoonful yielding as much as five ounces of milk, and is for this reason a better sweet for growing children than ordinary sugar or corn syrup when the amount of milk which they can have is limited, or when fruits and vegetables are hard to get. Molasses ginger snaps make, therefore, an excellent sweet for children, much better than candy, but of course to be eaten only at meal time.

The aim of good home cooking should be to please the family with what they ought to eat. The chef in a big hotel may have to prove the superiority of his art over that of a rival chef, and vie with him in novelty and elaboration, but the home cooking may be ever so simple provided the result is a happy, well-nourished family. A chocolate layer cake that takes two hours out of a day is no more nourishing than the same materials served as poached eggs, bread and butter, and a cup of chocolate. It is worth while to train a family to enjoy the flavor of simply prepared foods, and to realize that the food is the thing which counts and not the way it is dressed up. On the other hand, if one has to use a few food materials over and over, as one must in many places when the money that can be spent for food is very little, it is by slight changes in their form and flavor that one keeps them from palling on the appetite. If one has to use beans every day, it is a good thing to know a dozen different ways of preparing beans. One may have the plain bean flavor, properly toned up by a suitable amount of salt; the added flavor of onions, of tomatoes, of fat pork, of molasses, or a combination of two or three. One may have plain oatmeal for breakfast (the flavor developed by thorough cooking, at least three or four hours in a double boiler or over night in a fireless cooker); oatmeal flavored with apples in a pudding for dinner; or oatmeal flavored with onions and tomatoes in a soup for supper; the same food but quite different impressions on the palate.

Herbs and spices have from time immemorial given flavor to man's diet. "Leeks and garlic," "anise and cumin," "salt and pepper," "curry and bean cheese," are built into the very life of a people. The more variety of natural foods we have the less dependent we are upon such things. Our modern cooks, confronted in the present crisis with restrictions in the number of foods which they may use, may find in bay leaves, nutmeg, allspice, and all their kind, ways of making acceptable the cereals which make a diet economical, the peas and beans which replace at least a part of the meat, and dried fruits and vegetables which save transportation of fresh or canned goods.

Tea and coffee are both flavors and stimulants. They are used literally by thousands to give flavor to bread or rice. Dependence on a single flavor is apt to result in a desire to have it stronger and stronger, and hence less and less wholesome. This is a good reason for some variety of flavor; better tea one meal and coffee another than the same one all the time. Too freely used, and made too strong, tea and coffee may have a bad effect upon the nervous as well as the digestive system. They should never be given to children. It is better for adults to get their flavor from something without such effects. Because the combination of bread and coffee tastes good, one may be deceived into thinking himself well nourished on a diet consisting of little else. And yet this is a very inadequate diet for anybody, and disastrous to the normal development of children. One must be on guard, then, lest one's desire for flavor be satisfied without the body's real needs being met.

The wise cook saves her best flavors for the foods which would be least acceptable without them and does not add them to foods which are good enough by themselves. The latter course marks the insidious beginning of luxury. "Once give your family luxuries and you are lost as far as satisfying them economically is concerned," remarked a clever housewife. "Even a rat will not taste bread when bacon is nigh," observed a sage physiologist. The demand for flavor grows and grows with pampering, till nothing but humming-birds' tongues and miniature geese floating in a sea of aspic jelly will satisfy the palate of him who eats solely for flavor—who never knows the sauce of hunger, or the deliciousness of a plain crust of bread. We must be on guard, saying, like the little daughter of a classical professor, "If Scylla doesn't get me Charybdis will." Flavor we must have, but not too much, not too many kinds at once, and not applied indiscriminately to foods which need them and foods which do not. The wise cook uses her arts to secure the proper nourishment of the family and not for her fame as "a good cook."

CHAPTER VIII

ON BEING ECONOMICAL AND PATRIOTIC AT THE SAME TIME

Who does not sigh for the fairy table that comes at the pressing of a button? It is invariably laden with the most tempting viands, satisfies beyond words, and disappears when the meal is over, leaving behind no problem of leftovers or planning for the next meal! No money, no work, no thought, only sheer enjoyment. Alas, how different is the world of fact! Even if we have plenty of money we cannot escape from the thought of food today. There is imperative need for saving of food materials; at best there will not be enough to go around, and all the world, ourselves included, will suffer in proportion as we neglect the duty of food conservation. To be economical in the use of food materials according to the program of the Food Administration may, probably will, demand the spending of more money, time, and thought upon food. If we have the money and time to spend, well and good; but if we have not, how shall we do our share in sending more "wheat, meat, sugar and fats to our soldiers, sailors and allies"?

Thousands of people had to practice strict economy before the war began. They have no more money than they had then and the cost of food has increased. Certainly the first duty of everyone is to secure sufficient nourishment to avoid the undermining of health and strength which is sure to follow inadequate food. But we must all remember that it is possible to make a great many changes in diet without altering food value, and that there are few diets which cannot be so rearranged as to give a better nutritive return on the money spent than is usually secured by our haphazard methods of planning meals. Saving of waste is commendable and will go a long way, but this is a kind of passive service; loyal citizens ought to be active participants in the food conservation movement, which is a movement to distribute food in the way which shall promote the efficiency of our allies and ourselves in this world upheaval. To do this without increasing the cost of one's diet requires a careful study of the situation. No one can give precise rules as to how it shall be done, but perhaps a few suggestions as to the underlying principles will help in determining a dietary plan which shall be economical and still in line with the general policy.

The same nutritive essentials must be supplied whether the cost of the diet be much or little. A moderately active man needs some 3,000 calories per day whether his activity be playing golf or working on a farm; whether his board bill be $3.00 a day or $3.00 a week. In both cases there must be suitable kinds and amounts of protein-bearing food, of other "building materials," and those substances which directly or indirectly affect the smooth running of the body machinery; nevertheless, these two diets, closely alike in nutritive value, may be very dissimilar in their superficial appearance. For instance, all the nutritive requirements may be met in a ration composed of three food materials, as milk, whole wheat bread, and apples; on the other hand, by one composed of canvas-back duck, truffles, lettuce, celery, cranberries, white bread and butter, cream, coffee, and perhaps a dozen other items. We love all the various sensations that come from the mingling in a meal of food hot and cold, moist and dry, crisp and soft, sweet and sour, exhibiting the artistic touch as well as the homelier virtues; it is the sacrifice of pleasure of the esthetic sort that food economy and to some extent food conservation entail.

The first step in food economy (aside from saving of waste) is to emphasize the use of cereal foods. As much as one-fourth the food money may be invested in grain products without nutritive disadvantage. But this is not the last word on the subject, since cereal foods, while cheap, differ among themselves in cost and somewhat in nutritive value. It is possible to confine one's choice to some which contribute little besides fuel to the diet, such as rice and white flour, or to include those which are rich in other essentials, such as oatmeal. It is difficult to express briefly this difference in foods in any concrete fashion, but recently a method of grading or "scoring" foods has been introduced which may help to make clearer the relationship between nutritive value and general economy.

We cannot live exclusively upon foods which furnish nothing but fuel, though fuel is the largest item in the diet and one which in an effort to economize is apt to fall short; hence a food which furnishes nothing but fuel will not have as high a "score" as a food which will at the same time supply certain amounts of other essentials, such as protein, calcium (lime), iron, and the like. By giving definite values to each of the dietary essentials taken into consideration and comparing the yield of these from different foods, we may have such a score as follows:[1]

Grain products	Score value per pound
White flour	1,257
Graham flour	2,150
Rye flour	1,459
White bread	1,060
Graham bread	1,525
Cornmeal	1,360
Oatmeal	2,465
Cream of wheat	1,370
Hominy	1,147

[1] For the method of calculation and further data see "The Adequacy and Economy of Some City Dietaries" by H.C. Sherman and L.H. Gillett, published by The New York Association for Improving the Condition of the Poor, 105 East Twenty-second Street, New York City, from which these figures are taken.

Corn flakes   1,090

By comparing the score with the price per pound we can easily see which contributes most to the diet as a whole for the money expended. Thus, if hominy and oatmeal cost the same, the oatmeal is more than twice as cheap because we not only get a little more fuel from it but we also get protein, calcium, iron, and phosphorus in considerably larger amounts; that is, we shall need less of other foods with oatmeal than we shall with hominy. This does not mean that hominy is not an excellent and a cheap food, but it does mean that when the strictest economy must be practiced it pays to buy oatmeal. The task of the housewife is to find out how much she can make acceptable to her family; how much she can serve as breakfast food, how much in muffins and bread, how much in soups and puddings. This economy is strictly in harmony with the principles of food conservation—saving of wheat, so hard to do without entirely, so easy to dispense with in part.

Cornmeal gives as good a nutritive return per pound as cream of wheat, so that as long as the price of cornmeal is not higher than that of the wheat product it is both good economy and good patriotism to use it as far as one can. And, even if cornmeal should be dearer than wheat, one can save money by increasing the proportion of cereals in the diet so as to be able to be patriotic without increasing the food bill.

A second measure which generally makes for food economy is to emphasize the use of dried fruits and vegetables. The score of some of these foods almost speaks for itself:

Dried fruits and vegetables	Score value per pound
Beans	3,350
Peas	2,960
Apples	955
Dates	1,240
Figs	1,782
Prunes	1,135
Raisins	1,550

Fresh fruits and vegetables	
Beans	472
Peas	475
Apples	156
Bananas	236
Oranges	228
Peaches	138
Pears	228

From the foregoing it is evident that, unless the cost of a pound of fresh apples is less than one-fifth that of dried ones, the dried will be cheaper; that if dates and raisins cost the same per pound they are equally economical to buy. It may be noted, too, that the return on a pound of dried fruit may be quite as good in its way as the return on a pound of a grain product, but they will be equally cheap only when they cost the same per pound in the market. Here, again, there is no incompatibility between economy and conservation of special foods. Even in the case of beans is this true, for, while certain kinds are wanted for the army and navy, there are dozens of kinds of beans; one may count it as part of one's service to find out where these can be obtained, how they are best cooked and served. Soy beans commend themselves for their nutritive value, but how many American housewives have made them a part of their food program? How many have tried to buy them or asked their dealers to secure them?

A third step in the program of economy is the reduction of the amount of meat consumed. In many American families at least one-third the food money is spent for meat. That there are adequate substitutes which may be used to reduce the amount of meat bought has been already shown. Saving of meat is one of the most important planks in the food conservation program; so here again there is no inevitable conflict between conservation and economy. Some meat is desirable for flavor if it can possibly be afforded, but no economically inclined person should set aside more than one-fourth to one-fifth of the food money for it. How much one will get depends upon the kind and cut selected. There is not so much difference in the nutritive value as there is in the cost, as the following examples of "meat scores" will show:

Meat and fish	Score value per pound
Beef, lean round	1,664
Beef, medium fat rump	1,221
Beef, porterhouse steak	1,609
Veal, lean leg	1,539
Lamb, medium fat leg	1,320
Fowl	1,453
Codfish, salt	1,710
Codfish, fresh[*]	519
Salmon, canned	1,074

The great value of milk in the diet has already been discussed. The "score" of milk is about the same as that for sugar (milk, 761; sugar, 725); hence, if sugar is ten cents a pound and milk eighteen-cents a quart (about nine cents per pound), milk is cheaper than sugar. Yet there are people cutting down their milk supply when the cost is only thirteen or fourteen cents per quart on the ground that milk is too expensive! The economical housewife should have no compunctions in spending from one-fifth to one-fourth of her food money for this almost indispensable food. Whether the free use of milk will be good food conservation as well as good economy depends upon the supply. If there is not enough to go around, babies and the poor should have the first claim upon it and the rest of the world should try to get along with something less economical.

A pound of eggs (eight or nine eggs) gives about the same nutritive return as a pound of medium fat beef, but to be as cheap as beef at thirty cents a pound, eggs must not cost over forty-five cents a dozen. Eggs must be counted among the expensive foods, to be used very sparingly indeed in the economical diet. Nevertheless the use of eggs as a means of saving meat is a rational food conservation movement, to be encouraged where means permit.

The saving of sugar, while a necessary conservation measure, is contrary to general food economy, since sugar is a comparatively cheap fuel food and has the great additional value of popularity. Sugar substitutes are not all as cheap as sugar by any means, but molasses, on account of its large amount of mineral salts, especially of calcium, has a score value of 2,315 as against 725 for granulated sugar, and may be regarded with favor by those both economically and patriotically inclined.

In the case of fats, practical economy consists in paying for fuel value and not for flavor. The score values for butter, lard, olive oil, and cottonseed oil are about the same. The cheapest fat is the one whose face value per pound (or market cost) is the lowest. Fats are not as cheap as milk and cereals if they cost over ten cents per pound. The best way to economize is by saving the fat bought with meat, using other fats without much flavor, and cutting the total fat in the diet to a very small amount, not over two ounces per person per day. This is also good food conservation, since fats are almost invaluable in rationing an army, and those with decidedly agreeable flavor are needed to make a limited diet palatable.

No program either of economy or food conservation can cater to individual likes and dislikes in the same way that an unrestricted choice of food can. If one does not like cereals it is hard to consume them just to save money, especially to the extent of ten to fifteen ounces of grain products in a day. Yet one might as well recognize that in this direction the lowering of the cost of the diet inevitably lies. If one does not like corn, it is hard to substitute corn bread for wheat bread. But one might as well open one's mind to the fact that the only way to put off the day when there will be no white bread to eat is to begin eating cornmeal now. Most of us want to eat our cake and keep it too—to enjoy our food and not pay for our pleasure; to do our duty towards our country and not feel any personal inconvenience. But the magic table of the fairy tale is not for a nation at war; food is not going to come at the pressing of a button during this conflict. If we are to escape bankruptcy and win the war we must eat to be nourished and not to be entertained.

APPENDIX

SOME WAR TIME RECIPES

The following recipes illustrate some of the practical applications of the principles discussed in the foregoing pages. They have been selected from various publications, a list of which is given below. The numbers following the titles of the recipes correspond with the numbers of the publications in this list.

1. Canned Salmon: Cheaper than Meats and Why, U.S. Department of Commerce, Bureau of Fisheries, Economic Circular No. 11

2. Cheese and its Economical Use in the Home, U.S. Department of Agriculture, Farmers' Bulletin No. 487

3. Economical Diet and Cookery in Time of Emergency, Teachers College, Columbia University, Technical Education Bulletin No. 30 4. Food, Bulletin of the Life Extension Institute, 25 West 45th Street, New York City

4. Honey and its Uses in the Home, U. S. Department of Agriculture, Farmers' Bulletin No. 653

5. How to Select Food: Foods Rich in Protein, U.S. Department of Agriculture, Farmers' Bul'letin No. 824

6. Meat Substitutes, Connecticut Agricultural College, Emergency Food Series, No. 10

7. Ninety Tested, Palatable and Economic Recipes, Teachers College, Columbia University, Technical Educational Bulletin No. 34

8. Recipes of New York City Food Aid Committee, 280 Madison Avenue, New York City

9. Recipes in The Farmer's Wife, St. Paul, Minnesota, September, 1917

10. Some Sugar Saving Sweets for Every Day, Teachers College, Columbia University, Teachers College Record, November, 1917

11. War Economy in Food, Bulletin of the United States Food Administration

12. Waste of Meat in the Home, Cornell Reading Course for the Farm Home, Lesson 109

BREAD AND MUFFINS

Corn Meal and Wheat Bread (9)

- Corn meal, 1 cup
- Wheat flour, 2 cups
- Fat, 1 tablespoon
- Corn syrup, 1 tablespoon
- Salt, 1½ teaspoons
- Cold water, 1¼ cups
- Lukewarm water, ¼ cup
- Yeast, 1 cake

Pour cold water gradually over corn meal and salt. Cook over water for 20 minutes. Add fat and syrup. Allow to cool to room temperature. Add yeast which has been softened in the lukewarm water. Add flour gradually, stirring or kneading thoroughly after each addition of flour. Knead lightly for 10 or 15 minutes. Shape into a loaf. Let rise until double in bulk. Bake in a moderate oven (360-380°) for about an hour. (The amount of corn meal may be reduced if one desires a loaf with the characteristics of wheat bread.)

Corn Meal and Rye Bread (9)

- Lukewarm water, 2 cups
- Yeast, 1 cake
- Salt, ½ tablespoon
- Molasses, ½ cup
- Rye flour, 1 cup
- Corn meal, 1 cup
- Flour, 3 cups

Soften yeast cake in water, add remaining ingredients, and mix thoroughly. Let rise, shape, let rise again and bake.

Sour Milk Corn Bread (8)

- Corn meal, 1 pint
- Soda, ¾ teaspoon
- Baking powder, ¼ teaspoon
- Sour milk, 1 pint
- Salt, ½ teaspoon
- Egg, 1
- Lard (melted), 1 ½ tablespoons

Slightly beat the egg, add milk, salt, and soda. Stir in the meal. Beat well. Add melted lard and baking powder. Bake in hot greased pan. Cut in squares and serve. Do not have batter too stiff.

Eggless Corn Muffins (8)

- Corn meal, 1 cup
- Pastry flour (sifted), ½ cup
- Sugar, ¼ cup
- Melted butter, 2 tablespoons
- Salt, 1 teaspoon

- Baking powder, 2 teaspoons
- Milk, 1 cup

Mix dry ingredients and add milk and melted butter. Put in greased muffin pan and bake 30 minutes in a moderate oven.

Oat Bread (4)

- Boiling water, 2 cups
- Salt, ½ tablespoon
- ½ yeast cake, dissolved in ½ cup lukewarm water
- Rolled oats (dry), 1 cup
- Molasses, ½ cup
- Fat, 1 tablespoon
- Flour, 4½ cups

Add boiling water to the rolled oats, stir well and let stand for one hour. Add molasses, salt, fat, dissolved yeast cake, and flour; let the dough rise to double its bulk, beat well, and turn into greased bread pans, let rise the second time, and bake about one hour in a moderate oven.

Oatmeal Muffins (8)

- Cooked oatmeal, 1 cup
- Flour, 1½ cups
- Sugar, 2 tablespoons
- Baking powder, 4 teaspoons
- Salt, ½ teaspoon
- Milk, ½ cup
- Egg, 1
- Melted butterine, 2 tablespoons

Mix and sift flour, sugar, baking powder, and salt. Add the egg well beaten and one-half the milk. Mix the remainder of the milk with the cereal, and beat in thoroughly. Then add the butter. Bake in buttered muffin or gem tins about 30 minutes in a moderate oven.

War Time Boston Brown Bread

- Rye meal, 1 cup
- Corn meal, 1 cup
- Finely ground oatmeal, 1 cup
- Milk, 1½ cups
- Soda, ¾ teaspoon
- Salt, 1 teaspoon
- Molasses, 1 cup
- Baking powder, 2 teaspoons

Mix and sift dry ingredients, add molasses and milk, stir until well mixed, turn into a well-greased mold, and steam three and one-half hours. The cover should be greased before being placed on mold. The mold should never be filled more than two-thirds full. A one-pound baking powder box makes the most attractive shaped loaf for steaming; place mold on a trivet in kettle containing boiling water, allowing water to come half-way up around mold; cover closely and steam, adding as needed more boiling water. One cup chopped peanuts and 1 cup of cut dates may be added.

Rice Bread (10)

- Milk, ½ cup
- Sugar, 6 tablespoons
- Fat, 4 tablespoons
- Salt, 1½ teaspoons
- Compressed yeast, ½ cake, softened in ¼ cup liquid
- Boiled rice, 7 cups
- Flour, 8 cups

This proportion makes two loaves of bread.

Scald the milk with sugar, salt, and fat. Let cool until lukewarm and pour over the boiled rice. Add yeast which has been softened in one-quarter cupful warm water. Stir in flour and knead. Let rise until double its bulk. Knead again and put into pans. Let rise until light and bake 50 minutes to one hour in a moderate oven.

The rice should be boiled in a large quantity of boiling water, in order to insure a dry rice. At least eight or ten times as much water as rice should be used.

Eggless Rye Muffins (8)

- Rye flour, 2 cups
- Baking powder, 4 teaspoons
- Salt, ½ teaspoon
- Sugar, 4 teaspoons
- Milk, 1 cup
- Melted butter or other fat, 1 tablespoon

Mix and sift the dry ingredients; add the milk and melted fat. Mix quickly, do not beat. Bake in greased muffin pans 20 minutes in a hot oven.

Rye Corn Meal Muffins (9)

- Corn meal, ½ cup
- Rye flour, 1 cup
- Baking powder, 3 teaspoons
- Sugar, 2 tablespoons
- Melted butter, 1 tablespoon
- Salt, 1 teaspoon
- Milk, ¼ cup
- Egg, 1

Mix and sift dry ingredients, beat egg, add to it milk and molasses, then stir liquid mixture into dry ingredients. Do not beat. Place in well-greased muffin tins and bake in moderate oven 25 to 30 minutes.

Rye Rolls (9)

- Milk, 1 cup
- Water, 1 cup
- Fat, 3 tablespoons
- Sugar, 2 teaspoons
- Salt, 2 teaspoons
- Yeast cakes, 2
- Water, 6 tablespoons
- Rye flour, 4 cups
- White flour, 4 cups

Scald the milk with the salt, sugar, and fat. Soften the yeast in the six table-spoonfuls of water.

Cool the milk by adding the rest of the water cold, stir in the yeast and flour, and knead. Let rise until double in bulk. Knead again and shape into rolls. Let rise until very light and bake.

CAKE AND COOKIES

Apple Sauce Cake (4)

- Sugar, 1 cup
- Butter, 2 tablespoons
- Apple sauce, 1 cup
- Flour, 2 cups
- Raisins, ⅔ cup
- Soda, 1 teaspoon
- Cinnamon, ½ teaspoon
- Cloves, ½ teaspoon
- Salt, ¼ teaspoon
- Nutmeg, ¼ teaspoon

Sift together the soda, spices, salt, and flour. Cream the butter, add sugar, apple sauce, dry ingredients, and seeded raisins. Bake in a moderate oven.

Buckwheat Cookies (8)

- Butterine, ½ cup
- Sugar, 1 cup
- Eggs, 2
- Clove, ½ teaspoon
- Buckwheat, 1 ¾ cups
- Salt, ¼ teaspoon
- Cinnamon, ½ teaspoon

Beat the eggs, add the sugar and melted butter, and beat until thoroughly mixed. Sift the buckwheat, spices, and salt together and add very slowly. Mix well; roll on a floured board one-eighth to one-sixteenth inch thick. Cut the cookies and bake on a greased baking sheet in a moderate oven about 10 minutes.

Honey Bran Cookies (5)

- Bran, 3 cups
- Sugar, ½ cup
- Soda, ¼ to ½ teaspoon
- Cinnamon, ¼ teaspoon
- Ginger, ¼ teaspoon
- Honey, ½ cup
- Milk, ½ cup
- Melted butter, ½ cup

Soft Honey Cake (5)

- Butter, ½ cup
- Honey, 1 cup
- Egg, 1
- Sour milk, ½ cup
- Soda, 1 teaspoon
- Cinnamon, ½ teaspoon
- Ginger, ½ teaspoon
- Flour, 4 cups

Rub the butter and honey together; add the egg well beaten, then the sour milk and the flour sifted with the soda and spices. Bake in a shallow pan.

Molasses Cakes (4)

- Sugar, ½ cup
- Fat, ½ cup
- Molasses, 1 cup
- Ginger, 1 teaspoon
- Cinnamon, ½ teaspoon
- Egg, 1
- Flour, 2 ½ cups
- Soda, 2 teaspoons
- Hot water, 1 cup
- Salt, ½ teaspoon

Sift together the salt, sugar, flour, soda, and spices. Melt butter in hot water, add molasses, egg well beaten, and dry ingredients. Mix well. Bake in small cup cake tins in a moderate oven for about 25 minutes.

Molasses Cookies (11)

- Flour, 2¾ cups
- Salt, 1 teaspoon
- Soda, 1 teaspoon
- Ginger, 1 tablespoon
- Molasses, 1 cup
- Hot water, 1 tablespoon
- Hardened vegetable fat, ¼ cup

Sift together the flour, salt, soda, and ginger. Melt fat; add hot water and molasses; stir this liquid gradually into the dry ingredients. Chill. Roll on floured board to one-eighth inch thickness. Cut. Bake about 10 minutes in a moderate oven (360-380° F.).

Nut Molasses Bars (9)

- Oleomargarine, ¼ cup
- Hardened vegetable fat, ¼ cup
- Boiling water, ¼ cup
- Brown sugar, ½ cup
- Molasses, ½ cup
- Soda, 1 teaspoon
- Flour, 3⅔ cups
- Ginger, ⅓ teaspoon
- Cloves, 1/8 teaspoon
- Salt, 1 teaspoon
- Cocoanut, ½ cup
- English walnuts, ½ cup

Pour boiling water over fat; add sugar and molasses; add flour, soda, spices, and salt sifted together. Chill. Roll one-eighth inch thick. Cut in strips about three and a half by one inch. Sprinkle with cocoanut and English walnuts cut in small pieces.

Bake about 10 minutes in a moderate oven.

Oatmeal Cookies (4)

- Egg, 1
- Sugar, ¼ cup
- Milk, ½ cup
- Water, ¼ cup
- Flour, 2 cups
- Fine oatmeal, ½ cup
- Baking powder, 2 teaspoons
- Salt, 1 teaspoon
- Raisins, 1 cup
- Melted fat, 5 tablespoons

Sift together the flour, baking powder, and salt. Add the oatmeal. Beat the egg add sugar, water, and milk, dry ingredients mixed together, raisins, and melted fat. Drop from spoon on greased baking sheet and bake in moderate oven.

Oatmeal Macaroons (12)

- Fat, 1 tablespoon
- Corn syrup, 3/8 cup
- Sugar, 2 tablespoons
- Egg, 1
- Almond extract if desired, 2 teaspoons
- Oatmeal, 1 ½ cups

- Salt, ¼ teaspoon
- Baking powder, ½ teaspoon
- Flour, 1½ tablespoons

Combine the melted fat and sugar and syrup, add the beaten egg and stir in the other ingredients. Drop from a teaspoon on greased baking sheets or pans and bake in a moderate oven about 15 minutes.

Potato Drop Cookies (13)

- Hot mashed potatoes, 1½ cups
- Sugar, 1¼ cups
- Beef or mutton fat, 1 cup
- Flour, 1¾ cups
- Baking powder, 2 teaspoons
- Cinnamon, 1 teaspoon
- Cloves, ½ teaspoon
- Nutmeg, ½ teaspoon
- Raisins, chopped, ½ cup
- Nuts, chopped, ¼ cup

Combine the ingredients in the order given and drop the mixture by spoonfuls on a slightly greased tin. Bake the cookies in a moderate oven.

Spice Cake (9)

- Hardened vegetable fat, 3½ tablespoons
- Sugar, ¼ cup
- Egg, 1
- Corn syrup, ¼ cup
- Milk, ¼ cup
- Flour, 1 cup (plus 1½ tablespoons)
- Baking powder, 1¼ teaspoons
- Chopped citron, 2 tablespoons
- Raisins, cut in half, ½ cup
- Cinnamon, ¾ teaspoon
- Clove, ¼ teaspoon
- Nutmeg, 1/8 teaspoon

Cream fat; add sugar gradually, syrup, egg well beaten; mix and sift dry ingredients; add alternately with milk to first mixture. Add raisins (which have been rolled in a little of the flour), mixing them through the cake thoroughly.

Bake about 30 minutes in a moderate oven (about 380° F.).

JAMS AND SANDWICH FILLINGS

Banana and Nut Paste for Sandwiches (11)

- Banana, 1
- Shelled peanuts, ¼ cup

Mix the banana with the shelled peanuts, which have been crushed. Salt to taste. Use as a filling for sandwiches.

Carrot Marmalade (3)

- Carrots, 3 pounds
- Sugar, 3 pounds
- Lemon, 1 (juice and grated rind)
- Oranges, 2 (juice and grated rind)

Wash, scrape, and steam carrots until soft; chop fine and mix with fruit and sugar. Cook gently one hour.

Date and Cranberry Marmalade (3)

- Cranberries, 1 quart
- Dates, stoned, 1 pound
- Water, 1 pint
- Brown sugar, 2 cups

Simmer together for 20 minutes cranberries, dates, and water; put through a sieve; add sugar and cook 15 minutes longer.

Dried Apricot Conserve (11)

- Dried apricots, ½ pound (1⅔ cups)
- Cold water, 2 cups
- Raisins, 1 cup
- Juice of 1 lemon
- Whole orange, 1
- Nuts, ½ cup
- Corn syrup (light), 1 cup

Soak apricots over night in cold water. When soaked add raisins, lemon juice, orange sliced very thin, with slices cut in small pieces, and corn syrup. Bring to boiling point and simmer for about one and one-quarter hours. Add nuts 15 minutes before taking from fire.

Fruit and Peanut Butter (for Sandwiches) (11)

- Dates, ¼ cup
- Figs, ¼ cup
- Peanut butter, ½ cup
- Salt, ½ teaspoon
- Lemon juice, 1½ tablespoons
- Raisins, ¼ cup
- Corn syrup (light), 2 tablespoons

Wash figs, raisins, and dates, and put through food chopper. Add salt, peanut butter, lemon juice, and corn syrup, and mix well.

Plum Conserve (without sugar) (11)

- Pitted plums, 1 pound (2 dozen plums)

- Raisins, ⅓ pound
- Cold water, ½ cup
- Walnuts, 1/8 pound (¼ cup)
- Oranges, 2
- Corn syrup, ⅓ cup

Wash and cut plums in pieces: add chopped raisins, orange pulp and peel, cut very fine; corn syrup and water; boil until it is of the consistency of marmalade (about one and one-half hours of slow cooking). Add walnuts five minutes before removing from fire.

SUBSTANTIAL HOT DISHES

Baked Barley (4)

- Barley, ½ cup
- Boiling water, 3 cups
- Salt, ½ teaspoon
- Left over gravy, ¾ cup

Soak barley over night. Drain. Cook in boiling salted water until tender. Drain. Add left over gravy and bake for 20 minutes in a moderate oven. If one has a meat bone, or left over bits of meat, these may be boiled with the barley to give it flavor.

Beef and Bean Stew (6)

- Beef, lower round, 1 pound
- Red kidney beans, 1 cup
- Onion, 1
- Canned tomatoes, 1 cup, or 2 or 3 fresh tomatoes
- Salt pork, 2 ounces

Wash the beans and soak them over night. Cut the pork into small pieces and try out the fat. Cut the beef into small pieces and brown it in the pork fat, then add the vegetables with water enough to cover. Cook just below the boiling point for about three hours.

Cheese Fondue (2)

- Milk (hot), 1⅓ cups
- Bread crumbs, 1⅓ cups
- Butter, 1 tablespoon
- Eggs, 4
- Cheese, ⅓ pound (1⅓ cups grated or 1 cup cut in pieces)
- Salt, ½ teaspoon

Mix the water, bread crumbs, salt, and cheese; add the yolks thoroughly beaten; into this mixture cut and fold the whites of eggs beaten until stiff. Pour into a buttered dish and cook 30 minutes in a moderate oven. Serve at once.

Corned Beef Hash with Vegetables (4)

- Corned beef (cold, left over), 1½ cups

- Dice potatoes (cooked), 2¼ cups
- Turnips (cooked), 1 cup
- Onion, chopped fine, 1 small
- Carrots (cooked), ½ cup
- Water, ¾ cup
- Fat, 3 tablespoons

Cut the meat into small pieces. Add cooked vegetables cut into small cubes, onion and water. Put fat into hot frying pan, add hash and cook for about 20 minutes, allowing the hash to brown. Other left over meat may be added to corned beef, or used instead of corned beef.

Corn Meal Scrapple (3)

- Shin of beef, 2 pounds
- Salt, 1 teaspoon
- Onion, 1 medium
- Pepper, 1/8 teaspoon
- Cold water, 2 quarts
- Corn meal, 1 cup

Cook onion thinly sliced in beef marrow or suet. Add to water with meat and bone and cook until meat is tender. Let cool, skim off fat, and remove bone. To liquid remaining, add enough water to make one quart. Add corn meal and salt and cook one hour. Turn into a mold, cool, cut in slices, and fry in pork fat until brown. Serve with or without gravy.

Corn Chowder (4)

- Corn, ¼ can
- Salt pork, 1½ inch cube
- Potato cut in slices, 1 medium
- Milk, 2 cups
- Boiling water, 1½ cups
- Butter, 2 tablespoons
- Sliced onion, 1/8
- Sugar, ¼ teaspoon
- Salt and pepper

Cut the pork into small pieces and try it out. Add the onion and cook for about five minutes. Strain the fat into a stew pan. Cook the potatoes for about five minutes in boiling salted water. Drain, and add the potatoes to the fat. Add the boiling water and cook until the potatoes are soft. Then add corn and milk and heat to the boiling point. Add the salt, pepper, sugar, and butter. Serve immediately after adding butter.

Cottage Cheese and Nut Loaf (12)

- Cottage cheese, 1 cup
- Nut meats (use those locally grown), 1 cup
- Stale bread crumbs, 1 cup

- Juice of ½ lemon
- Salt, 1 teaspoon
- Pepper, ¼ teaspoon
- Chopped onion, 2 tablespoons
- Oleomargarine, meat drippings or vegetable oils, 1 tablespoon

Mix the cheese, ground nuts, crumbs, lemon juice, salt, and pepper. Cook the onion in the fat and a little water until tender. Add to the first mixture the onion and sufficient water or meat stock to moisten. Mix well, pour into a baking dish, and brown in the oven.

Dried Fish Chowder (7)

- Salt fish, ½ pound
- Potatoes, cut in small pieces, 4 cups
- Salt pork, 2 ounces
- Small onion, chopped, 1
- Skim milk, 4 cups
- Crackers, 4 ounces

Salt codfish, smoked halibut, or other dried fish may be used in this chowder. Pick over and shred the fish, holding it under lukewarm water. Let it soak while the other ingredients of the dish are being prepared. Cut the pork into small pieces and fry it with the onion until both are a delicate brown; add the potatoes, cover with water, and cook until the potatoes are soft. Add the milk and fish and reheat. Salt, if necessary. It is well to allow the crackers to soak in the milk while the potatoes are being cooked, then remove them, and finally add to the chowder just before serving.

Gevech (Roumanian Recipe) (9)

- Shredded cabbage, 1¼ cups
- Chopped onion, ¼ cup
- Rice, ¼ cup
- Diced potatoes, ¾ cup
- ½ green pepper cut into strips
- Fish, ¾ pound
- Canned tomato, ¾ cup
- Water, 3 tablespoons
- Salt, ¾ teaspoon
- Paprika, ¼ teaspoon
- Pepper, 1/8 teaspoon

Parboil cabbage, onion, rice, potatoes, and green pepper together in salted water for 20 minutes. Drain. Clean fish, cut into small pieces, and mix with parboiled vegetables, canned tomatoes, water, and seasonings. Bake in a moderate oven for about 40 minutes. Baste occasionally while cooking. Serve with a garnish of sliced lemon.

Kidney Bean Stew (3)

- Kidney beans, 1 cup
- Onion, 1 small
- Rice, 2 tablespoons
- Canned tomatoes, 2 cups
- Fat or drippings, 2 tablespoons
- Flour, 2 tablespoons
- Salt and pepper to taste

Soak beans over night in cold water to cover. In the morning place beans over fire, adding water to cover if necessary. Add onion, rice and tomatoes and cook slowly until beans are soft. If too thick, add water. Mix flour and fat, and use to thicken stew.

Baked Oatmeal with Cheese (9)

- Cooked oatmeal, 4 cups
- Grated cheese, 1 cup
- Salt and pepper
- Soft bread crumbs, ¼ cup
- Fat, 1 teaspoon

Put into an oiled baking dish a layer of left over oatmeal, then a sprinkling of grated cheese, pepper and salt, another layer of oatmeal, then cheese and seasonings; continue until the dish is full. Melt the fat and mix with this the bread crumbs. Sprinkle over the top of the dish. Bake in a moderate oven until the crumbs are golden brown.

Green Pea Loaf with White Sauce (9)

- Dried green peas, 1 cup
- Cold water, 4 cups
- Boiling water, 2 quarts
- Soft, stale bread crumbs, 1½ cups
- Milk, 1½ cups
- Salt, 1 teaspoon
- Pepper, 1/8 teaspoon
- Paprika, ½ teaspoon
- Grated onion, ½ teaspoon
- Egg, 1
- Fat, 3 tablespoons

Soak peas in cold water over night. Cook in boiling water until soft. Rub through a sieve. To one cup of this pea pulp add bread crumbs, milk, seasoning, egg (slightly beaten), and melted fat. Turn mixture into a small, oiled bread pan. Set pan into a second pan, containing water. Bake mixture 40 minutes or until firm. Remove loaf from pan. Serve with white sauce. One-half cup of cheese may be added to one and one-half cups of the sauce.

Mock Sausage (8)

- Lima beans, dried, ½ cup

- Bread crumbs, ⅓ cup
- Butter, 3 tablespoons
- Egg, 1
- Pepper, few grains
- Salt, ¼ teaspoon
- Sage, ½ to ¾ teaspoon

Pick over and wash beans, cover with water, and let soak over night. Drain; cook in boiling salted water until tender, about one and one-half hours. Force through a strainer, add remaining ingredients. Shape into form of sausages, roll in crumbs, egg, and crumbs again. Sauté in fat until brown. It requires about two-thirds cup crumbs and one-half egg for dipping sausage. May be garnished with fried apples.

Baked Soy or Togo Beans (6)

Soy beans, known in the retail market as togo beans, resemble navy beans in some ways. They contain, however, a considerable amount of fat. For this reason neither pork nor other fat is used in cooking them unless it is wanted for flavor. They are considerably richer in protein also.

Wash and pick over one quart of soy beans. Cover with boiling water, boil for 10 minutes, and soak over night in the same water. In the morning pour off and save the water. Pour cold water over the beans and rub them between the hands to remove the skins, which will float off in the water. Removing the skins in this way takes only two or three minutes and greatly improves the quality of the dish. If a few skins are left on, they will do no harm, unless the dish is being prepared for a person of poor digestion. Drain the beans, pour over them the water in which they were soaked, and cook until tender at a temperature just below the boiling point. Pour off the water, put the beans into a bean pot, cover with cold water, add one and one-half tablespoonfuls of salt, and bake four or five hours in a covered dish. Remove the cover and bake one hour more.

Peanut Loaf (10)

- Chopped peanuts, 1 cup
- Bread crumbs, 2 cups
- Egg, 1
- Milk, 1 cup
- Salt, 1½ teaspoons
- Paprika, ¼ teaspoon
- Melted fat, 1 tablespoon

Mix dry ingredients, add beaten egg and milk. Put into a greased pan, pour the melted fat on top, bake. Turn on a hot platter and serve with sauce.

Sauce for Loaf

- Hot water, 1 cup
- Beef cube, 1
- Juice 1 lemon

- Fat, 2 tablespoons
- Flour, 2 tablespoons
- Salt, ½ teaspoon
- Paprika, 1/8 teaspoon
- Few grains nutmeg

Melt fat, add flour with seasoning, add hot water in which beef cube has been dissolved. Just before serving add lemon juice.

This nut loaf with its accompanying sauce is a highly nutritious dish and is excellent for lunch or supper. Serve no meat or potatoes with it.

Peanut Butter Bean Loaf (10)

- Peanut butter, ½ cup
- Cooked beans, 1 cup
- Soft bread crumbs (toasted), 1 cup
- Milk, 1 cup
- Salt, 1 teaspoon
- Pepper, ½ teaspoon

The beans should be soaked over night and cooked in fresh water until tender. Press through a sieve, add other ingredients, mix well. Shape into a loaf, place in pan, and bake about two hours, basting with melted fat and hot water.

Peanut Butter Cream Soup (10)

- Milk, 1 quart
- Onion (grated), 1 small
- Flour, 1 tablespoon
- Melted fat, 1 tablespoon
- Peanut butter, 1 cup
- Bay leaf, 1
- Celery (chopped) 3 stalks
- Celery salt, 1 saltspoon
- Salt, ½ teaspoon
- A little white pepper
- Dash of paprika

Heat milk in a double boiler, add peanut butter, onion, bay leaf, chopped celery, and other seasoning. While the milk is heating, melt fat in a separate sauce pan, stirring in flour as for cream sauce. When smooth add the hot milk, after straining through a sieve. Serve at once with croutons or tiny squares of bread browned till crisp.

Peanut Fondue (8)

- Peanuts, shelled, 1 cup
- Bread crumbs (soft), 1 cup
- Milk, 1⅔ cups
- Egg, 1
- Salt, 1½ teaspoons

- Cayenne

Grind peanuts in a meat grinder. Mix all ingredients except the white of the egg. Beat the egg white stiff and fold in. Turn into a buttered pudding dish and bake in a moderate oven 30 to 35 minutes.

Peanut Soup (10)

- Blanched shelled peanuts, 2 cups
- Onion, ¼ cup
- Celery, ¼ cup
- Carrot, ¼ cup
- Water, 2½ cups
- Fat, ¼ cup
- Flour, 2 tablespoons
- Salt, 1 teaspoon
- Paprika, ½ teaspoon
- Milk, 2 cups

Chop and crush the nuts until very fine; add the vegetables and water; simmer 20 minutes. Make a white sauce of the other ingredients, mix the two mixtures thoroughly and serve.

Potato Soup with Carrots (4)

- Potatoes, 3 medium
- Water, 2 cups
- Flour, 4 tablespoons
- Soup greens
- Onion, 2 slices
- Sprigs of parsley
- Milk, 1½ cups
- Carrot, 1
- Fat, 1½ tablespoons
- Salt and pepper
- Stalk of celery

Wash and pare potatoes. Cook in boiling salted water until they are soft. Rub through colander. Use water in which potatoes were cooked to make up the two cups of water for the soup. Cook carrot cut in cubes in boiling water until soft; drain. Scald milk with onion, celery, and parsley. Add milk and water to potatoes. Melt fat in sauce pan, add flour, and cook for three minutes. Slowly add soup, stirring constantly. Boil for one minute, season with salt and pepper. Add cubes of carrots and serve.

Salmon en Casserole (1)

Cook one cup of rice. When cold line baking dish. Take one can of salmon and flake. Beat two eggs, one-third cup of milk, one tablespoon of butter, pinch of salt, dash of paprika. Stir into the salmon lightly, cover lightly with rice. Steam one hour, serve with white sauce. (This may also be made with barley instead of rice.)

Scalloped Salmon (1)

- Salmon, 1 can
- Egg, 1
- Milk, 1 pint
- Flour, 2 rounding tablespoons
- Butter, 1½ tablespoons

Put the milk on stove in double boiler, keeping out one-half cup. Mix butter and flour to a smooth paste, and add the egg well beaten, then the one-half cup of cold milk. Mix well and then stir into the milk, which should be scalding. Stir until smooth and thick like gravy. Season with salt and pepper and set aside to cool. Butter a baking dish and fill with alternate layers of flaked salmon and the cream dressing. The top layer should be of the dressing. Sprinkle with cracker crumbs and bake one-half hour in moderate oven.

Salmon Loaf (1)

- Salmon, 1 small can
- Egg, 1
- Cracker crumbs, 1 cup
- Sweet milk, 2 tablespoons
- Paprika
- Nutmeg
- Salt

Remove bones from salmon; break into small pieces, add well beaten egg, seasoning, and cracker crumbs; bake in a well buttered dish for 15 minutes; serve hot for lunch.

Tamale Pie (12)

- Corn meal, 2 cups
- Salt, 2 ½ teaspoons
- Boiling water, 6 cups
- Onion, 1
- Fat, 1 tablespoon
- Hamburger steak, 1 pound
- Tomatoes, 2 cups
- Cayenne pepper, ½ teaspoon,or
- Chopped sweet pepper, 1 small
- Salt, 1 teaspoon

Make a mush by stirring the corn meal and one and one-half teaspoons salt into boiling water. Cook in a double boiler or over water for 45 minutes. Brown the onion in the fat, add the Hamburger steak, and stir until the red color disappears. Add the tomatoes, pepper, and salt. Grease a baking-dish, put in a layer of corn meal mush, add the seasoned meat, and cover with mush. Bake 30 minutes. Serves six.

Turkish Pilaf (3)

- Washed rice, 1 cup
- Raw lean beef or lamb, 1 pound
- Salt, 1 teaspoon
- Boiling water, 2 cups
- Small onion or garlic, 2 cloves
- Tomatoes, 2 cups
- Olive oil or any fat, 2 tablespoons

Fry onion cut in small pieces or the garlic in the fat until slightly brown; add rice, seasonings, water, tomatoes, meat, and cook in a covered dish until the rice is soft. The meat may be omitted, the rice cooked in the tomatoes and water, and the whole covered with grated cheese and baked until cheese is melted.

Vegetable Stew

- Beef, ½ pound
- Mutton, ½ pound
- Carrots, diced, ½ cup
- Potatoes, diced, 2 cups
- Tomatoes, canned, ¾ cup
- Fat, 2 tablespoons
- Carrot, 1 whole
- Onion, sliced, 3 tablespoons
- Cabbage, chopped, 1 cup
- Flour, ¼ cup
- Bay leaf, ½ leaf
- Cloves, 6
- Peppercorns, 6
- Parsley, chopped, 2 tablespoons
- Salt, 2 teaspoons
- Thyme, 1 sprig
- Water, 7 cups

Cut meat in small pieces, brown with onion in fat, add water, one carrot in which cloves have been imbedded, and other vegetables. Tie bay leaf, thyme, and peppercorns together in a piece of cheesecloth and cook with stew about two hours (till vegetables are done). Remove bag of seasonings, thicken stew with flour. Add more salt if needed.

PUDDINGS

Apricot Tapioca Pudding (4)

- Apricots, 6
- Sugar, ½ cup
- Pearl tapioca, 1 cup
- Salt, ½ teaspoon
- Boiling water, 3 cups

Cover the tapioca with cold water and soak for one hour. Drain off the cold water, add the boiling water and salt, and cook over water (in a double boiler if you have one) until the tapioca is transparent, and no hard center portion remains. This will require about 30 minutes. Place the apricots in a buttered baking dish. Add sugar to the tapioca, pour this over the apricots, add apricot juice, and bake in a moderate oven for about 20 minutes. Cool and serve. If dried apricots are to be used, they should be soaked over night or several hours in cold water sufficient to cover them. Cook in the water in which they have soaked until they are tender.

Cereal Pudding (8)

- Left over cereal, 3½ cups
- Apple sauce, ½ cup or
- Apple, 1
- Sugar, 1 tablespoon
- Butter, 1 tablespoon
- Bread crumbs, 2 tablespoons

Put a layer of cereal in the bottom of a buttered baking dish, then a layer of apples or sauce, then sugar if the sauce has not been sweetened. Then put in another layer of cereal, cover with buttered crumbs. Bake 30 minutes if it has apple sauce in it, one hour if raw apples are used. Serve with cream.

Cereal Date Pudding (11)

- Cereal (half corn meal and half farina), ¾ cup
- Boiling water, 3 cups
- Salt, ¾ teaspoon
- Chopped dates, 1 cup
- Oleomargarine, 1 tablespoon
- Corn syrup (light), ½ cup
- Egg, 1

Stir the cereal mixture gradually into the boiling water, to which the salt has been added. Cook directly over the flame for about five minutes, stirring constantly, and then cook over water for one and one-half hours. Add oleomargarine, syrup, egg, well beaten, and chopped dates. Turn into a greased baking dish and bake for about 30 minutes in a moderate oven (360-390° F.).

Chocolate Bread Pudding (11)

- Bread, broken in small pieces, 2 ½ cups
- Corn syrup (dark), ½ cup
- Brown sugar, ¼ cup
- Egg, 1
- Salt, ¼ teaspoon
- Chocolate, 2 squares
- Milk, 1 ½ cups
- Hot water, 1 ½ cups
- Vanilla, ¾ teaspoon

Soak bread in milk; add syrup, brown sugar, egg, well beaten, and salt. Melt chocolate in water; add gradually to bread mixture. Add vanilla. Bake in custard cups, set in hot water, in a moderate oven.

Eggless Steamed Pudding (11)

- Flour, 1⅔ cups
- Soda, ½ teaspoon
- Salt, ¼ teaspoon
- Cloves, ¼ teaspoon
- Allspice, ¼ teaspoon
- Nutmeg, ¼ teaspoon
- Cinnamon, ½ teaspoon
- Hardened vegetable fat, 3 tablespoons
- Molasses, ½ cup
- Milk, ½ cup
- Raisins (seeded and cut in pieces), 1 cup

Sift together the flour, soda, salt, and spices; add the raisins. To milk add molasses and melted fat; add liquid mixture gradually to dry ingredients. Stir thoroughly. Turn into greased molds, filling them a little over half full; cover and steam for about two and one-half hours. Serve with pudding sauce or milk. (Baking powder cans are satisfactory molds for steamed puddings.)

Honey Pudding (5)

- Honey, ½ cup
- Bread crumbs, 6 ounces
- Milk, ½ cup
- Rind of half a lemon
- Ginger, ½ teaspoon
- Eggs, 2
- Butter, 2 tablespoons

Mix the honey and the bread crumbs and add the milk, seasonings, and yolks of the eggs. Beat the mixture thoroughly and then add the butter and the whites of the eggs well beaten. Steam for about two hours in a pudding mold which is not more than three-quarters full.

Indian Pudding (3)

- Milk, 1 quart
- Molasses, ½ cup
- Corn meal, ⅓ cup
- Ginger, 2 teaspoons
- Salt, 1 teaspoon
- Cold milk, 1 cup

Pour milk, scalded, over meal, and cook 20 minutes; add salt, ginger, and molasses. Cook slowly in a buttered baking dish two hours. When half done, add the cold milk and finish cooking.

Baked Indian and Apple Pudding (8)

- Corn meal, ¼ cup
- Milk, 2 cups
- Salt, ½ teaspoon
- Ginger, ½ teaspoon
- Molasses, ¼ cup
- Apple, 1

Sift corn meal slowly into the scalded milk, stirring constantly. Cook in double boiler 30 minutes, stirring occasionally. Add salt, ginger, and molasses. Put into greased baking dish and bake one hour in a slow oven, stirring occasionally. Slice apple and stir into pudding. Bake until apple is tender.

Prune Brown Betty (11)

- Cooked prunes, stoned and cut into halves, 2½ cups
- Bread crumbs (dry), ½ cup
- Corn syrup (dark), ¼ cup
- Lemon juice, 3 tablespoons
- Grated rind of ¼ lemon
- Cinnamon, ¼ teaspoon
- Salt, ½ teaspoon
- Oleomargarine, 1 tablespoon
- Prune juice, ½ cup

Mix together heated prune juice, fat, salt, corn syrup, lemon juice, lemon rind, and cinnamon. Moisten bread crumbs with part of this mixture. Into a greased baking dish put alternate layers of bread crumbs and prunes, pouring part of liquid mixture over each layer of prunes. Bake in a moderate oven about 45 minutes.

Rice Pudding (11)

- Rice, ¼ cup
- Milk, ¾ cup
- Corn syrup (light), 2 tablespoons
- Nutmeg, ¼ teaspoon
- Raisins, ¾ cup

Cook the rice in boiling salted water, until soft. Pour off water, add milk, syrup, nutmeg, and raisins. Bake in a moderate oven (370-380° F.) for 40 minutes.

Spiced Pudding (11)

- Browned crusts of bread, 1 cup
- Scalded milk, 2 cups
- Molasses, ½ cup
- Raisins, ½ cup
- Salt, ½ teaspoon
- Nutmeg, ¼ teaspoon
- Cinnamon, ¼ teaspoon
- Cloves, ¼ teaspoon

Soak the crusts in the milk until soft. Add molasses, salt, spices, and raisins.

Bake in a moderate oven (360-380° F.), stirring occasionally at first. Serve with milk or cream.

ENDNOTES

[*]   The low score of fresh cod is due chiefly to the absence of fat and the presence of water.

Lector House believes that a society develops through a two-fold approach of continuous learning and adaptation, which is derived from the study of classic literary works spread across the historic timeline of literature records. Therefore, we aim at reviving, repairing and redeveloping all those inaccessible or damaged but historically as well as culturally important literature across subjects so that the future generations may have an opportunity to study and learn from past works to embark upon a journey of creating a better future.

This book is a result of an effort made by Lector House towards making a contribution to the preservation and repair of original ancient works which might hold historical significance to the approach of continuous learning across subjects.

HAPPY READING & LEARNING!

LECTOR HOUSE LLP
E-MAIL: lectorpublishing@gmail.com